Essential Church History

Essential Church History

And the Doctrinal Significance of the Past

ADAM MURRELL

RESOURCE *Publications* · Eugene, Oregon

ESSENTIAL CHURCH HISTORY
And the Doctrinal Significance of the Past

Copyright © 2011 Adam Murrell. All rights reserved. Except for brief quotations in critical publications or reviews, no part of this book may be reproduced in any manner without prior written permission from the publisher. Write: Permissions, Wipf and Stock Publishers, 199 W. 8th Ave., Suite 3, Eugene, OR 97401.

Resource Publications
An Imprint of Wipf and Stock Publishers
199 W. 8th Ave., Suite 3
Eugene, OR 97401
www.wipfandstock.com

ISBN 13: 978-1-61097-077-8

Manufactured in the U.S.A.

Unless otherwise indicated, all Scripture quotations are from The Holy Bible, English Standard Version® (ESV®), copyright © 2001 by Crossway, a publishing ministry of Good News Publishers. Used by permission. All rights reserved.

For my family,
Always reforming

Contents

Introduction ix

1 The Canon of Scripture (*c.* 1400 BC–AD 95) 1
2 Persecution in the Early Church (64–313) 32
3 The Arian Controversy (318–381) 49
4 Augustine of Hippo and the Pelagian Controversy (354–430) 63
5 The Crusades (1095–1291) 79
6 In Quest for Reformation (1305–1516) 92
7 The Protestant Reformation (1517–1648) 110
8 The Church in North America (1607–Present) 129

Appendix I—Dating the Books of the Bible 145
Bibliography 147

Introduction

CHURCH HISTORY. FEW OTHER topics have had as many books written about it—so why yet another one? Though there are many detailed accounts of the church throughout the ages, beginning with Luke's narrative of the early church (Luke-Acts) and continuing to the present, few approach the historical narrative account from the perspective of *sola Scriptura*. This little work provides an overview of how the Bible was first inspired, canonized, and preserved, and then takes the reader on a journey throughout seminal moments in the life of the church to discover what happens when the principle of *Scripture alone* is abandoned, and conversely, what transpires when the Bible is petitioned. The story of the church is filled with countless tales of believers vulnerable to heresy, schism, and false doctrines, because they were functioning without an adequate base in defense of their way—the Bible. This book will show how essential God's Word was in maintaining doctrinal integrity and harmony within the visible church, how it brought comfort to the weary, and how it proved sufficient to correct aberrant teachings. Here is a story that is both old and new.

The story of Christianity is old. Its history has been told and retold across the globe for the past two millennia. A voluminous stream of literature has been penned over the centuries, detailing its aspect in one form or another, and for good reason. The influence of Christianity on the world is a reality that simply cannot be denied. The truth is that life itself is measured in reference to Jesus of Nazareth—though political correctness of recent years has attempted to suppress this reality. The chronological record is measured against the life of Christ as BC (before Christ), and AD (*Anno Domini*), the year of our Lord. It is not surprising, therefore, to discover both students and scholars alike have endeavored to understand the nature of the church and have attempted to disseminate its history for all posterity.

The story of Christianity is also ever new. It must be told afresh in each age and not merely because a new chapter is added by the ongoing events of the present. With each new generation, believers are able to gain a fresh perspective of the past and build upon those experiences. They are able to follow the examples of men and women as they obeyed Christ, as well as learn from previous mistakes. But more than this, each generation must rise up and embrace the church's teachings personally. When theological doctrines are merely passed along without the recipients being firmly convinced of its veracity, apathy oftentimes prevails, and the resolve to fight for key tenets of the faith is lacking. Christians must exercise the God-given ability to study and to learn what Francis Schaeffer called "true truth". Meaning, while we do not have exhaustive truth from the Bible, we do, however, possess true truth about God, true truth about man, and something truly about nature. So on the basis of Scripture, we have true and cohesive knowledge. Divine truths are, indeed, given to God's people, while the gospel message is "veiled only to those who are perishing" (2 Cor 4:3). So for all of the aforementioned reasons, history and the Bible must be explored thoroughly in order for one to come to a greater clarity of and appreciation for what believers in the past endured, and also to come to a position of strong faith.

Essential Church History (ECH) is an attempt to bridge these important subjects in an effort to provide believers with lessons from the past, while presenting the overarching theme inherent in the story of the church. The aim in each of these topics is to demonstrate that God has worked in and through a peculiar people throughout the ages to preserve his truths by bringing every thought captive to the Word of God and subjecting every doctrine to that which is ultimately God-breathed. As the church accomplishes this fundamental task by remaining faithful to her heritage, she will continue to persist in truth. However, when such practice is abandoned, egregious error permeates the visible church and drowns out truth for a season.

As the title suggests, this book is only a skeleton of the past two millennia, and it is in no way intended to be a complete synopsis of church history. Such a compendium would be nearly impossible to compile. Essential events and personages have been selected in chronological order for the purpose of communicating a recurring theme throughout the history of the church: The Bible stands preeminent, and only when people adhere to the God-breathed Scriptures are they able to function and practice in line with his truth. But more than this, one will also discover how the Scriptures enabled believers to stand firm during difficult times and how it served as the bedrock of their faith, bringing hope and encouragement in a world fraught with peril.

The primary purpose for this book—originally a series of lectures delivered in a Sunday school setting, with a few personal convictions sprinkled in for good measure—is theological in nature. That is to say, while ECH is principally a historical narrative of the church, it was written in order to communicate the importance of the Christian's ultimate authority in all matters pertaining to faith and practice. Without such, believers are left like a ship on the sea without a rudder. They are tossed here and there and everywhere.

The moments described herein will reflect what happens when that rudder, the Bible, is forsaken. The reader will also discover in each instance that the only way in which theological perversion was even recognizable was when faith and practice were compared with Scripture. Returning to God's written revelation was the only way in which reformation happened, something that was necessary from the earliest times and continued throughout church history. The well-known tenet of the Protestant Reformation, *semper reformanda*, always reforming, is more than just a slogan—it should be a way of life for the church in every generation.

ECH was also written to induce the reader to study in fuller detail the people and events that shaped the church. From the process of canonization to the church's role in shaping the society of North America, ECH draws out the absolute necessity of understanding the integral role of the Bible. Furthermore, each chapter provides an instructive lesson for believers regarding how they might live and function in a society that oftentimes is hostile to the idea of absolute truths. To that end, I hope you will find this little book on church history beneficial for its historical narrative as well as the doctrinal significance contained in each section.

—Adam Murrell
King George, Virginia
October, 2010

1

The Canon of Scripture

(c. 1400 BC–AD 95)

How can we believe in the God of Christianity if we don't even know whether the Bible is trustworthy? The number of Americans asking this question is skyrocketing. Liberal influences have steadily been on the rise, gaining prominence within mainline Christian denominations. Skepticism, fear, and frustration toward traditional Christianity are growing in power and influence—including dissatisfaction from a number of regular churchgoers.

Though there is, in my opinion, unassailable proof to answer this perennial question adequately, many people have sought to dismantle the authority of Scripture from what they perceive to be a lack of tangible evidence. Challenges concerning the reliability of the Bible are increasingly prevalent in our postmodern society and deserve our attention. Much of the attacks are pouring in from more than just academic elites. In short, assaulting God's Word is seemingly in vogue these days.

One of the most influential books of recent years contributing to this mounting cynicism toward the reliability of the New Testament was written by popular fiction writer, Dan Brown. Indeed, the most provocative piece of literature that cultivated seeds of growing skepticism concerning traditional Christian teachings was the creative work of a novelist from New Hampshire with his mega-bestseller, *The Da Vinci Code*—a book whose message is still shaping viewpoints in many respects. Various aspects of the novel are probably as fresh in the minds of people today as when the book was first released.

Anyone who is old enough to remember will agree the novel's publication created a firestorm of controversy in which both believers and historians were united in opposing many aspects of the book's historical accounts. Compelling as it is as a murder mystery, the images created from Brown's work paints a picture that does not accurately represent the facts of history. In fact, in matters pertaining to Jesus, Mary Magdalene, Constantine, and the New Testament, the book was, to speak candidly, good fiction but most often short on fact. Here are just a few of the many historical problems with the book:

1. The Dead Sea Scrolls were not "found in the 1950s" (p. 234). The year was 1947.
2. Neither were the Dead Sea Scrolls among the "earliest Christians records" (p. 245); the scrolls are Jewish.
3. The Nag Hammadi documents do *not* tell the story of the Grail at all, nor do they emphasize Jesus' humanity—quite the opposite, in fact.
4. The Q document is not a surviving source hidden somewhere in the Vatican. The Q document is merely a hypothetical manuscript that scholars have posited as having been available to Matthew and Luke.[1]

And that's just a start. From there, the historical whoppers increase. Consider.

The story begins with the mysterious murder in Paris of the Louvre's curator. Left behind at the scene of the crime are peculiar religious symbols drawn by the victim himself just prior to his own demise. Robert Langdon, Harvard professor and renowned expert on symbology, was lecturing in Paris on the night of the crime and, by good fortune, was available to be called on to help investigate the murder and explain the mysterious clues. What Langdon eventually uncovers is a centuries-old conspiracy to suppress the "truth" of the historical Jesus.

Langdon ultimately discovers the real Jesus had a love affair with Mary Magdalene, who is pregnant with child at the time of the crucifixion—a fact known by the early church but concealed. This information was, at one time, widely available and even recorded in the Gnostic gospel of Mary, but the church had all conflicting gospels and documents destroyed.

---

1. For a listing of factual errors in *The Da Vinci Code*, see Ehrman, *Truth and Fiction in The Da Vinci Code: A Historian Reveals What We Really Know about Jesus, Mary Magdalene and Constantine*, xiv–xv.

According to Brown, Constantine the Great and officials at the Council of Nicea financed a "new" Bible—the Scriptures as we know of them today. During the selection process, the emperor chose only a few gospels (out of the eighty something that were purportedly in contention) that spoke of Jesus' deity and embellished the facts. Afterward, the Christian Scriptures gradually evolved, thanks in part to substantial emendations and revisions.[2] These allegations, among others, are just a few of the many distortions of history Brown proffers as being faithful representations of past events.

While some might easily and discernibly recognize the manifest folly of Brown's thesis, the poignant reality is that for many people *The Da Vinci Code* is history. And to some extent, with the approbation of a few within modern liberal circles, such conclusions are gaining support. So-called academicians have followed suit, albeit to a lesser degree, and joined in the chorus of imputing orthodox Christian tenets to Constantine and his council in the early fourth century. Thus, they hold that major tenets of the Christian faith were formed for political calculations and not resulting from theological convictions grounded in established truths.

But the reality stands at open variance with the "Da Vinci Code" crowd. To the dispassionate witness, the truth is far from Dan Brown's distortions. Among the copious writings penned in the aftermath of Brown's novel, one can find a host of writings from evangelicals to secular historians who respond to his factual errors. Yet, while a spate of books was released in the wake of the novel in order to correct the misrepresentations suggested in the mega-bestseller, the reality is that most people will never discover the truth behind the fiction. Numerous assertions have been made, and most people will never take the time or make the effort to sort out truth from error.

Not only is the church compelled to contend against egregious historical accusations from fiction writers (among many others), Christians must also compete with the rampant skeptical presuppositionalism that asserts the Bible cannot be trusted as history. Indeed, the majority of biblical scholarship has seemingly jettisoned the doctrine of inspiration and assumes the Scriptures are nothing more than influential Near Eastern literature. For many scholars, reading the Bible is merely an exercise in literary criticism, analogous to approaching any other ancient document.

2. See Brown, *The Da Vinci Code*, 231–34.

In so doing, the world of academia has reduced God's Word to mutually-exclusive writings from a host of bigoted, misogynistic, and sexually-repressed men (most notably, Paul) who are fueled by religious zeal, albeit myopic. Moreover, whereas the approach of the "Jesus Seminar"—whose scholars concluded the New Testament is propaganda from the earliest Christians—was once deemed radical, the methodologies employed are now gaining influential repute in a drastically gullible world.

Such postmodern skepticism, epitomized in *The Da Vinci Code*, provides a lucid reminder why every Christian is duty-bound to be able to provide an answer for the hope contained within. In order to withstand the perpetual assault from Brown and those who stand in concert with him, the evangelical must take these perennial issues seriously and be able to recognize truth from error and articulate a reasoned defense. Being able to accomplish this is not some task reserved for the elders of the church alone. Rather, it is an essential element for any professing believer.

Though, in the event Christians become despondent over "Da Vinci Code" attacks, Dan Brown perhaps said it best himself when he pointed out that the church has withstood heresy, schism, and other pernicious influences so an author from New England (speaking of himself) is not going to overthrow the Christian religion. Indeed, he is accurate in this assessment. Still, his perpetuation of already discredited arguments should force Christians into recognizing attacks on the Christian faith are not thinning out. Instead, they are growing exponentially from a number of avenues.

So what is the solution? The easiest approach to counter such criticisms is to understand church history. Christians must be prepared to reason with those ignorant of the past. Scripture is filled with repeated warnings concerning the real and present danger of false teachers and deceivers. We must be able to give a defense on the most basic level, starting with the foundation of our faith—the Bible.

THE MEANING AND ORIGIN OF THE CANON

The term "canon," borrowed from the Greek *kanon*, is simply a way of saying a rule or a measuring rod. So if we were to extend this term to the Bible, the canon of Scripture deals with the body of literature that meets the standard for inclusion to function in the church as the measuring rod for believers. Since the fourth century, the term canon has been used to denote authoritative books belonging to the Old and New Testaments.

The Canon of Scripture

Summarizing the *London Baptist Confession of 1689*, the declaration expressed the canon this way: The Holy Bible is the only certain and infallible rule of all saving knowledge, faith, and obedience that constitutes salvation. What this means is the canon of Scripture is *the* rule for the church—because it is from God. Understanding the nature of the Bible will provide the believer with a solid foundation upon which to stand firm against a host of attacks regarding its sufficiency and inerrancy.

The classic text used to demonstrate these elements of Scripture is found in Paul's second epistle to Timothy. This passage is arguably the primary reference in the affirmation of the sufficiency of the Bible alone, and by logical extension, the inerrancy of Scripture as well. The apostle is here delivering one final exhortation. Of all the messages he could have chosen to communicate just prior to his imminent demise, Paul wrote these concluding words of exhortation:

> "But as for you, continue in what you have learned and have firmly believed, knowing from whom you learned it and how from childhood you have been acquainted with the sacred writings, which are able to make you wise for salvation through faith in Christ Jesus. All Scripture is breathed out by God and profitable for teaching, for reproof, for correction, and for training in righteousness, that the man of God may be competent, equipped for every good work" (2 Tim 3:14–17).

Notice Paul's teaching concerning the nature of the Bible. He reveals that sacred Scripture is *theopneustos* (a combination of *theos*, meaning "God," and *pneō*, meaning "to breathe, blow"), which literally means "God-breathed" or "breathed out from God." That is to say, the text of Scripture is the product of the divine, life-giving breath of the Almighty—breathed out through the secret operation of the Holy Spirit by which he produced the Word of God from the word of men. All human authors were powerfully guided and led to write his message by divine initiative yet without suppressing the individual personality of each writer. Consequently, the words penned by each author, while under inspiration from the Spirit, are not only free of fault and error but also relay a message of supreme value for humanity. After commenting extensively regarding the significance of the word *theopneustos* (used only once in Scripture), the late Princeton theologian Benjamin B. Warfield (1851–1921) summed up the term by indicating the Scriptures owe their origin to an activity of God the Spirit, and as such, are in the highest and truest sense his creation.

Now to say God creates by the "breath of his mouth" is not unique to the formation of the Bible. The manner in which the world was created was identical. Creation, the other "book" that testifies to the reality of God was, according to the psalmist, made by the breath of his mouth (Ps 33:6). Indeed, by the word of the Lord the heavens were made. So, too, were human beings given life. God formed Adam from the dust of the earth and breathed the breath of life into him so that he became a living being and soul. Similarly, God breathed his Word, the Scriptures, into existence through human instruments. They are just as much a part of his creation as the universe or humanity, and because of this certainty, are being preserved.

Moreover, the mere fact that the Bible represents God's voice guarantees that it is profitable in the Christian life and for the work of the ministry for Christ's bride, the church. When Paul delivers these final words of encouragement to Timothy, he is telling him that he is not alone. God has not left the church unattended but has provided for her the Word of God. Paul is stating that all which is *theopneustos* will prove profitable for training in righteousness so that the man of God may be fully equipped, complete for every good work. And all of this is derived, not from unwritten, vacillating human traditions but from the Bible alone.

All in all, that which is ultimately breathed out by God has no higher authority, because there can be nothing greater than the very words of God. Hence, it is sufficient because it is, as the apostle stated, the breath of God. It is well worth the effort here once again to point out that Paul said all Scripture is God-breathed and not merely portions of it—which would include all books that would eventually become inscripturated.

Peter likewise confirms the inauguration of Scripture as coming from God. He writes, "For no prophecy was ever produced by the will of man, but men spoke from God as they were carried along by the Holy Spirit" (2 Pet 1:21). With the beginning remarks, Peter demolishes any pretension that Scripture originated with mankind. Instead, prophecy comes from God. More specifically, the Holy Spirit employed men to compose the words of God while still preserving their individual talents, insights, thoughts, feelings, emotions, and characteristics, yet keeping them from fault or error. The power of the Spirit was upon each author as they spoke and wrote and even enabled them to declare the grandeur of their work. David testified to this reality when he proclaimed, "The Spirit of the LORD speaks to me; his word is on my tongue" (2 Sam 23:2).

To understand the ultimate origin of the Bible is to recognize that humans wrote the Bible as they were moved along by the Spirit, just as Peter affirmed. He guided their writings so that they conveyed the very message of God and not thoughts of their own. The words of the apostles and prophets are authoritative and binding on the conscience of the believers, because the source of revelation derived from God. And that revelation spanned nearly a millennium and a half, including more than forty authors from the time of Moses to the days of the apostle John with books written in the Hebrew (with some Aramaic) and Greek languages.

Despite the diversity of authorship and length of time it took to complete the canon, we have one continuous and harmonious book that is first among all others. The Holy Bible is the measuring rod by which all norms are to be judged, the means by which God revealed his will regarding salvation, and outlines the duties he requires of us. Put another way, the Bible is the medium by which God speaks to his creation, so it is on this foundation of divine origin, as B. B. Warfield rightly concluded, that all the high attributes of Scripture are built.

THE EMERGENCE OF THE OLD TESTAMENT CANON

The Jews possessed a special reverence for Scripture. They expressed this sentiment in an exceptional way. Seeking to place a hedge of protection around the Law, the Jews required a man to undergo a meticulous process to remove uncleanliness before and after he touched the holy books. This made it difficult even to take the words of God within the hands. As cumbersome as this practice was, the tradition later expanded to all the sacred writings.

To the modern reader this practice might seem rather peculiar. It is challenging for many of us to imagine a rigorous devotion to an object, let alone ponder the holiness of something. Yet, this is exactly what the Jews did. They were capable of understanding that they had in their possession something sublime. God's chosen people were able to recognize that which ultimately came from him because of the testimony of the Holy Spirit. It's really that straightforward.

It might sound almost too simple to be verifiably true, but the reality is that the same Spirit who carried along holy men to write God's Word also revealed to his people the extent of the canon. The Holy Spirit guided the saints living under the Old Covenant to discover what was truly from God. Indeed, this idea is confirmed by Paul when he stated the "Jews were entrusted with the oracles of God" (Rom 3:2). By so doing, the apostle corroborated the reality that the New Testament church was not created in a vacuum but that it was the extension and fulfillment of the promises given to Abraham. The earliest Christians, therefore, were bequeathed the Jewish Scriptures. The church did not create the Old Testament canon nor did she grant authority to it. Instead, the church was given a definitive collection of books preserved by the Jewish people—books whose authority and divine origin were discernable in contrast to other non-inspired writings.

Another instructive aspect to consider it that God communicated his truths to humanity via the use of words. It was his intent to convey a particular message to his people. The fact that God desired to speak to mankind at all provides credence to the idea that the same God who first moved to correspond with us is the same God who equips us with the capacity to recognize and to understand his divine message. Jesus said, "My sheep hear my voice, and I know them, and they follow me" (John 10:27). God guided Israel in being able to discern his voice—and later the New Testament church—in recognizing that which is ultimately God-breathed.

As Christians, then, we can all possess confidence in the God who is there who communicates his Word to us. Though some have suggested an infallible human authority is first necessary in order to know the contents of the canon, the reality is that we must arrest the temptation to think of God in such diminutive terms. Instead, we must learn to trust in the efficacious power of a sovereign Holy Spirit to illumine God's people properly, guiding them into truth.

This divine illumination to the body of believers is clearly demonstrated in the Israelites' recognizing the voice of God when Moses read to them the "book of the covenant" (Exod 24:7). This phrase typically refers to the Ten Commandments and the Covenant Code found in chapters 20–23. Even during the life of the prophet Moses, the Book of the Law was considered sacrosanct as it was put "by the side of the ark of the covenant" (Deut 31:26) to serve as a reminder to the people of the commands of God binding upon them.

Beyond this, Moses is frequently cited as having been active as a writer, recording the words of the Lord commanded by him (Exod 17:14; 24:4; 34:27; Num 33:2; Deut 31:9, 19, 22; 24–26). In 2 Kings 22–

23, Hilkiah finds the "Book of the Law" and gives it to the king to read, after which he "tore his clothes" (22:11). That is, the king recognized the words of God, just as the people did when it was read in their hearing. The king and the Jewish people, convicted through the Book, made a covenant before the Lord to walk after him and to keep his commandments (23:1–3).

Later prophets also recognized their divine calling and understood their message contained authority because of its origin. The Bible makes clear that the prophets recorded their message—sometimes without explicit divine command and other times writing it down after being instructed to do so by God (Isa 30:8; Jer 25:13; 29:1; Ezek 43:11; Hab 2:2); at times recording dreams and visions (Dan 7:1–2); and even receiving letters from other prophets whose message was discernibly from God (2 Chron 21:12).

In light of the evidence that God's written Word was, at varying times, uncovered by the Israelites who were supposed to pass down these teachings, and if ever there was an object lesson that was learned during the reign of Josiah, it was that oral traditions could easily be forgotten or forsaken. Perhaps the greatest example of this truism is the fact that it was not until Hilkiah discovered the Book of the Law that great shock permeated the Israelites when they eventually uncovered what they were already supposed to know. The permanence, therefore, was not in the oral tradition but in the written form of God's message. So it is to the latter that we now turn to discover its history.

Though the Pentateuch (the first five books of the Bible) has been generally attributed to the hand of Moses, it is hard to say exactly how much of Genesis, Exodus, Leviticus, Numbers, and Deuteronomy, as we possess them in their final form today, were written by the prophet. For instance, prophets who succeeded Moses in mediating the divine message (cf. Deut 18:15–22) presumably kept the text updated both historically and linguistically, adding material such as Genesis 14:14 where Abraham pursued Lot's captors as far as Dan, however the place did not receive this name until after the Danites captured the area following the Conquest (Josh 19:47; Judg 18:29). Then too, later prophets added Genesis 36:31 and Moses' obituary as recorded in Deuteronomy 34. Others critical of full Mosaic authorship have pointed out that there exists among the five books a diversity of material, namely vocabulary, syntax, style and general composition differences—most notably when comparing the law codes as found in Leviticus and Deuteronomy. Further examples include various uses of the divine names Yahweh ("Lord") and Elohim ("God") in Genesis and Exodus, which, it is suggested, points to a later amalgamation of several documents.

A final argument against full Mosaic authorship is duplications and triplications of material that are not easily resolved by simply appealing to "doublet passages". This phrase refers to the Hebraic form of literature wherein a set of two or more words (or constructions) might occur together and refer almost essentially to the same (synonymous or nearly synonymous) action, quality, or entity (e.g., the creation accounts in Genesis 1 and 2).

Be that as it may, what must be kept in mind is not to subscribe dogmatic statements to the Bible that the text itself does not support. The Pentateuch as a whole is an anonymous work. Moses is never mentioned explicitly as the author of the five books, apart from references to his writing down of historical facts (Exod 17:14; Num 33:2), laws or sections of law codes (Exod 24:4; 34:27–28.), and even a poem (Deut 31:22). While Jesus and the apostles also affirmed the common belief of their day that Moses wrote Scripture (Mark 7:10; 10:3–5; 12:26; Luke 5:14; 16:29–31; 24:27, 44; John 7:19, 23), the corpus of writings by Moses is not demonstrably set forth in the text of Scripture. That is to say, the degree to which Moses wrote the five books as we possess them today is unknown, because the evidence lends support to an extended transmission and development. Nevertheless, as more than one scholar has concluded, the evangelical can stand confident in his belief that Moses' role in the production of the Pentateuch must be affirmed, as the prophet was highly instrumental in its formative stages—although it remains questionable whether or not he wrote the Pentateuch as it survives today.

Stated another way, it is likely that the Pentateuch was the effort of a single author (Moses) but later went through an editing process after his death. In the final analysis, however, whichever side one chooses to take in this discussion, the Christian must bear in mind that the thrust of the legislative material and narrative account must, without question, be reckoned as authentic.

Setting aside the question of human authorship now—since literary activity in the ancient Near East was commonly anonymous—what must be kept in mind is the process by which books are recognized as being authoritative is not always immediate. Sometimes it took generations before certain literature was known and accepted collectively as divine. While we have internal evidence within the Pentateuch that parts of it were understood to be canonical, other sections of the five books did not achieve the same status at exactly the same time. The revelatory process was not always immediate nor was it lucidly attested.

What is known and accepted without dispute, however, is the Pentateuch was completed and reckoned canonical no later than the time of Ezra and Nehemiah in the fifth century BC. The schism between the Jews and Samaritans during the intertestamental period also lends support to the belief that the Pentateuch was canonical by the time of the last prophet in that both parties embraced the first five books.[3]

Those five books of the Hebrew Bible are in the same order as our Old Testament is today. The rest of the Hebrew canon, however, is different from Christian Bibles—in number of books and order, but not in content. The traditional rendering of the Hebrew canon is composed of twenty-four books, although some writers tended to group the works differently to arrive at twenty-two. So, for instance, Kings, Samuel, the Minor Prophets, Chronicles, and Ezra-Nehemiah are all reckoned as a single book. The remaining structure of the Hebrew Bible is divided into two further sections: the Prophets and the Writings (Hagiographa). The former comprised eight books, which included: Joshua, Judges, Samuel, Kings, Jeremiah, Ezekiel, Isaiah, and the Twelve (the Minor Prophets). The third and final division of the Hebrew canon, the Writings, was comprised of eleven books, namely, Psalms,[4] Job, Proverbs, Ecclesiastes, Song of Songs, Lamentations, Daniel, Esther, Ezra-Nehemiah, and Chronicles.

The period for recognizing the authority of these latter two sections of the Hebrew Bible—much like the dating of the Pentateuch—is disputed. Suspicion has sometimes been cast, though without compelling reason, on the antiquity of these groupings. Skeptics have alleged that the grouping of the canon of the Prophets was hastily closed without properly including books such as Daniel and Chronicles (which, they

---

3. It is often suggested only the Pentateuch was recognized as canonical by the time of the split between the Jews and Samaritans, because the latter only accepted the Pentateuch. A. C. Sundberg, however, argues that the restriction to the Pentateuch by the Samaritans involved a conscious effort to exclude the prophets. See Sundberg, *The Old Testament of the Early Church*, 111. Also Bruce, *The Canon of Scripture*, 41.

4. In the traditional order, Ruth is a preface to Psalms and was only later moved in order.

allege, naturally belong their and not to the Writings). The canon of the Writings, in following this increasingly popular theory, was not officially closed until the so-called Jewish synod of Jamnia about AD 90. According to this hypothesis—one which Roman Catholics vigorously defend for obvious reasons—the New Testament church did not inherit a closed canon, but instead, embraced an open canon of Scripture. This broader canon purportedly embraced by the New Testament church was embodied in the Greek version of the Old Testament (the Septuagint, also called LXX), which it is assumed, contained the Apocrypha.[5]

As interesting as this speculation might initially appear, the theory is without much historical merit. While no evangelical consensus can be reached regarding the specific dates that the authoritative status was reached, it is highly dubious to suggest an open canon following the life of Christ. In fact, the totality of the evidence strongly suggests a closed canon containing the traditional twenty-two books at least a couple of centuries prior to the ministry of Jesus. We see specific references confirming this reality in ancient literature which refer to "the Law and the Prophets and the others" as found in the prologue of the second-century BC book of Sirach, among other intertestimental works.[6] Here we have explicit proof that a tripartite Jewish canon existed no later than the time in which Sirach was penned. But this is not the only evidence in support of a three-fold division prior to the life of Christ. Let's consider some other testimony.

Maccabean tradition speaks about a great crisis during the second century before Christ: "Judas [Maccabaeus] collected all the books that had been lost on account of the war which had come upon us, and they are still in our possession" (2 Macc 2:14). The "war" of which he speaks concerns the Maccabean war for liberation against the Syrian oppressor, Antiochus Epiphanes. Once the persecution ended, Judas gathered the copies and, knowing that prophecy had ceased long before his time (1 Macc 9:27), he compiled the complete collection of writings and set them in the traditional Hebrew order. Since the books were still in the form of scrolls,

---

5. But even this theory of a larger Alexandrian canon has many problems. There is no evidence any canon existed outside the Palestinian canon. Moreover, Codex Sinaiticus, our oldest complete Greek Bible, does not contain all the apocryphal books Rome defined as canonical at the Council of Trent. So there does not even seem to be a consensus as to which apocryphal books were recognized as authoritative, if any at all, by some in the early church.

6. Schnabel, "History," 16–24.

Judas gathered them all, provided a firm division between the Prophets and Writings, and rendered the number at twenty-two. This number is elsewhere affirmed by other canonical and non-canonical writings.

Third, the Jamnia hypothesis has been under assault by modern scholarship because our knowledge of what actually happened is limited. There is no indication that the meeting was anything more than a gathering to discuss already accepted books, let alone a full and comprehensive synod. As best as anyone can speculate, the Apocrypha was never discussed, and there is no indication that any previously held books were excluded.

Fourth, Josephus, the first century Jewish historian writing in the first volume of his treatise, *Against Apion*, bears testimony to a fixed canon during the intertestamental period. There, he spoke of the Hebrew Bible consisting of only twenty-two books, comprised of the traditional threefold division: the Law, the Prophets, and Writings (which are equivalent in content to the Protestant Old Testament of today).

In addition to all the external evidence for a closed canon by the end of the first century BC (if not earlier), presumably the greatest and definitive testimony regarding a closed canon by the time of Christ was the division he enumerated. While many have sought to confuse the issue regarding the completion of the Old Testament, there is sufficient internal evidence to provide us with a lucid picture of Jesus functioning in his day with a closed Old Testament, provided we let the plain testimony of Scripture speak for itself. Beginning in Luke, we read:

> "Therefore this generation will be held responsible for the blood of all the prophets that has been shed since the beginning of the world, from the blood of Abel to the blood of Zechariah, who was killed between the altar and the sanctuary" (Luke 11:50–51, NIV).

Jesus is here referring to the structure of the traditional Hebrew Bible. When Christ spoke of Abel to Zechariah, he was pointing out the first and the last prophets to be murdered. That is, Abel's death is recorded in Genesis, while Zechariah is cited in Second Chronicles—the first and last books of the Jewish canon. Also, on the road to Emmaus, Luke again records what Jesus and the apostles viewed as canonical. "And beginning with Moses and all the Prophets, he explained to them what was said in all the Scriptures concerning himself" (Luke 24:27). Again, the general description of using the traditional division of "Moses" (or Law),

"Prophets," or "Psalms" as Jesus did in Mark 12:10 designate the tripartite division of Bible. Jesus' hearers would have undoubtedly understood to what books he was referring.

Indeed, Jesus was familiar with the same Old Testament canon of which the apostles used and understood. So, too, were the Pharisees; and all of Jesus' hearers knew what he meant when he repeatedly asked, "Have you not read?" Here we see Jesus expecting his listeners to know what was in the canon and held them accountable for its contents. Would it have done the Pharisees any good to answer back, "But we aren't sure precisely which books belong in the canon, so how can you rebuke us?" No, of course not; arguing so would be absurd. The canon was known in Palestine during the time of Christ. Jesus functioned as if it was closed, and no one gives testimony to the contrary. All the evidence we can muster, from literature of the intertestamental period to the words of Jesus himself, gives us a clear indication that a Hebrew canon existed during his day consisting of the Law, the Prophets, and the Writings.

DOES THE APOCRYPHA BELONG IN THE OLD TESTAMENT CANON?

It should come as no surprise that when the Roman Catholic and Protestant Bibles are compared, there is a great disparity between the Old Testaments. It is no secret that Roman Catholics include a number of works in the Old Testament commonly referred to as the Apocrypha or the deuterocanonical Scriptures. The exact number of books (and additions to several canonical books of Scripture) varies depending on how one counts them. Sometimes listed at fourteen or fifteen, the Apocrypha includes Baruch, Judith, First and Second Maccabees, Sirach (Ecclesiasticus), Tobit and Wisdom, as well as some accompaniments to Daniel and Esther. Combined, these works amount to approximately two-thirds the size of the entire New Testament. Since this is a matter of dealing with such a vast amount of literature, which introduces concepts foreign to the rest of Scripture (e.g., Purgatory, prayers for the dead), it goes without saying that recognizing the full subject matter of the Bible is no trivial matter.

As has already been pointed out, Josephus lists the exact books belonging to the Hebrew canon (the same as Protestant Bibles), and Jesus also delimits the inclusion of any apocryphal literature. In addition to these witnesses, there are even more sources that point to a fixed Old Testament canon devoid of the deuterocanonical writings.

Philo of Alexandria (c. 20 BC–AD 50) is another witness who is interesting to note and must be dealt with on a historical level when discussing canonical matters. He was, as one scholar has summed up, the apotheosis of Alexandrian Judaism, so his conclusions should not be dismissed easily, nor should they be disregarded without compelling reason.[7] What is gripping about his life and testimony is that he was only familiar with the Greek version of the Bible, the LXX (the same one which purportedly contained the Apocrypha). Yet, he affirmed the traditional division of the Hebrew Bible—Law, Prophets, and Writings—but gave no sign of accepting the Apocrypha as authoritative (books that some allege were part and parcel of the Septuagint).

Even though Roman Catholic apologists argue for the worldwide acceptance of apocryphal books contained in the Greek Bible, Philo does not support the narrative of Rome's allegations. If ever there were a representative who could testify to the authenticity of the deuterocanonical Scriptures, it would have been the Jewish philosopher, Philo, but we do not have any evidence for believing this.

Rabbinical literature from the early centuries after Christ also provides a key piece of information in understanding the division and content of the Hebrew Bible. One of the clearest statements regarding the threefold division of Jewish Scriptures is found in the tractate *Baba Bathra* in the Babylonian Talmud. This passage provides us with knowledge regarding the makeup of the early Jewish writings and demonstrates the canonical status during the first century did not include the Apocrypha. Again, we see how the documents of antiquity fail to provide support for the inclusion of any additional books outside the Hebrew (Protestant) Old Testament.

And let's not forget about Aquila, the early second century Jewish proselyte—a man whose credentials in learning have never been in dispute. One of his most profound contributions to posterity was his revised Old Testament. He labored under the daunting task of translating the Hebrew Scriptures into Greek in the early years of the second century after the Jews became disenchanted with the Christians' usage of the Septuagint. Working under the auspices of the Palestinian Jewish leaders, Aquila completed his monumental endeavor in which he fol-

---

7. See discussion in Bruce, 44–46.

lowed the traditional reckoning of the Old Testament, excluding any and all apocryphal literature.

There is yet another significant witness to this threefold division of the Hebrew canon. This one, nonetheless, is found in the prologue to Ecclesiasticus, one of the apocryphal books (written c. 130 BC). Amazingly, the writer understands there are three specific groups of books which are authoritative. What is important to note is that he does not even begin to hint that Ecclesiasticus (his own work) should belong to any of the three traditional categories (Law, Prophets, or the rest of the books). So the question one needs to consider is: How can the Roman Catholic Church claim Ecclesiasticus (and other apocryphal writings) belongs to the Old Testament canon when the book itself delimits its own authority? If the writer acknowledges a tripartite division is already in existence, then Ecclesiasticus clearly cannot belong to any one of the particular categories. This means that if the divisions and contents thereof were already defined before Ecclesiasticus was even written how, then, can one seriously argue Ecclesiasticus belongs to one of the divisions? The answer, I submit, is obvious—one cannot consistently do so.

Another telling point to consider comes from the apocryphal book of First Maccabees. In several instances the author mentions there was no prophet in the land at the time of his writing (4:46; 9:27; 14:41). Understanding this is essential because, as we might recall from earlier, Peter indicates, "knowing this, first of all, that no prophecy of Scripture comes from someone's own interpretation. For no prophecy was ever produced by the will of man, but men spoke from God as they were carried along by the Holy Spirit" (2 Pet 1:20–21). Following the death of Judas Maccabeus (190 BC–160 BC), prophets and the spirit of prophecy had ceased to exist in the land of Israel. Since a prophet must be living in order to receive sacred Scripture, and Maccabeus confirms there were no prophets, the author also eliminates his own work from canonical contention. Stated simply, without a prophet there can be no inspired writings.

Not only does the historical record fail to indicate support for the inclusion of the Apocrypha, prevalent and manifest errors are telling as well. Without even touching upon the common theological contradictions often cited against the deuterocanonical books—because one can always allegorize or spiritualize a text and thus explain away an obvious contradiction—one must not overlook historical discrepancies that cannot be subjected to allegorizing or whatever other attempt one chooses to employ.

Indeed, while theological misstatements can, albeit with defective elasticity, be stretched so as to harmonize an apparent contradiction, historical statements must be assessed at face value. That is, if any apocryphal writer makes historical statements, we can easily ascertain the veracity of such declarations by comparing statements to known facts.

For instance, the apocryphal book Judith makes the historical claim, "In the twelfth year of the reign of Nabuchodonosor [Nebuchadnezzar], who reigned in Nineve, the great city; in the days of Arphaxad, which reigned over the Medes in Ecbatane . . ." (Jdt 1:1). Just a few verses later, however, in verse seven, the author writes, "Then Nabuchodonosor [Nebuchadnezzar] king of the Assyrians . . ." The problem with these statements is that the historical and biblical evidence does not comport with these assertions. Nebuchadnezzar was, in fact, the king of Babylon—not of Assyria—and did not rule from Nineveh. The editors of the New Jerusalem Bible—the Catholic translation bearing the *Nihil obstat* and *Imprimatur*—likewise judge these verses to be factually erroneous.[8] The New Jerusalem Bible concludes, ". . . [H]istorically he was king of Babylon and was never styled 'king of Assyria,' and Nineveh was not his capital city." This rather basic historical fact should have been readily available to the writer (cf. 2 Kgs 24:1), and yet he persisted in committing a fundamental blunder. So in the final analysis, Roman Catholic and evangelical scholars alike stand united—at least in this instance—in recognizing some fundamental inaccuracies in elements of apocryphal literature.

A second fallacious statement worth noting appears in the testimony of Baruch, also an apocryphal work. There, the author purportedly wrote the words of the book while in Babylon, during the time Nebuchadnezzar burned Jerusalem (Bar 1:1–2; Jer 52:12–13). However, the prophet Jeremiah places Baruch in Egypt at the very time he was supposedly writing in Babylon (Jer 43:6–7). Clearly, then, both accounts, which contain contradictory statements about the past, cannot be accurately portraying history.

---

8. The *Nihil obstat* and *Imprimatur* are a declaration that a book or pamphlet is considered to be free from doctrinal or moral error. Upon this basis, then, it is also reasonable to conclude their judgments concerning historical facts should be viewed as highly trustworthy.

In another apocryphal book, Tobit records that he lived to be "an hundred and eight and fifty years old" (14:11), yet, apparently he was alive when Jeroboam revolted (931 BC) and also when Assyria conquered Israel (722 BC). The problem is obvious for anyone who takes time to calculate the simple math. The events spoken of are separated by a span of greater than two hundred years—several decades longer than his purported lifespan of 158 years. And these are just a few of the many problems inherent in the apocryphal literature.[9]

The Jews—those to whom the Word of God had been entrusted—regarded the Apocrypha as falling outside the canon. Though attractive in recounting historical events, displaying proper attitudes of Jewish piety, demonstrating resoluteness and suffering, and some laudable teachings on justice, morality, and religious obligations, the Jewish people did not accept the apocryphal literature as sacred Scripture. It must be remembered that the Jews were the ones to whom the church looked regarding the oracles of God. The Jewish people—those who comprised the earliest churches—brought with them a closed canon consisting of twenty-two (or twenty-four) books, the same Old Testament recovered during the Protestant Reformation.

THE EMERGENCE OF THE NEW TESTAMENT

The Old Testament was written over a period of more than one thousand years. The New Testament, by contrast, was completed within the span of a single century. Yet, even though the inscripturation process was produced more quickly than the Old Testament, the development of the New Testament canon is a long and complicated story that demands specialized study regarding the final list and arrangement. While we find a broad outline of the New Testament fixed no later than the mid-second century, local and differing traditions remained. Eventually, several features came to the fore and believers (the church) eventually united on what was canonical.

This recognition of many of the New Testament books was exponentially more rapid than that of the Old. In fact, God's people recognized the inherit authority of some books soon after they were recorded, just as the Jews had done earlier with some of their writings. Indeed, the

---

9. For a fuller discussion of the Apocrypha, see Webster, *The Old Testament Canon and the Apocrypha*; Whitaker, *Disputations on Holy Scripture*; and Murrell, *So You Want to Become a Roman Catholic?*

recognition of the majority of the canon was known during the earliest periods. By the time of Paul's first letter to the Thessalonians—postulated by some to be the earliest Pauline book of the New Testament—he compared his own message to "the word of God" (2:13) and commanded Christians to read his exhortations. "I put you under oath before the Lord to have this letter read to all the brothers" (5:27). Elsewhere, he speaks of his words as a "command of the Lord" (1 Cor 14:37). This personal testimony is confirmed by Peter who had no compunction to include Paul's writings with the other books of Scripture (2 Pet 3:15–16).

What is also telling in 1 Timothy 5:18 is the formula Paul chooses when he writes, "For the Scripture says . . ." He follows that introduction with a quote from Deuteronomy 25:4 (cf. Luke 10:7) and the phrase, "The laborer deserves his wages," a quote from Matthew 10:10. By prefacing the verses in the manner he did, Paul unequivocally gave equal importance to the New Testament Gospel. Clement of Rome (d. 101), considered the first of the Apostolic Fathers, also testifies to the authority of Matthew and Luke in which he freely acknowledges their importance and shows an intimacy with many of the Pauline letters in his own correspondence to the Corinthian church in AD 95. Two other early church Fathers, Polycarp and Ignatius, combined with Clement, authenticated the New Testament Scriptures by referring to them as authoritative. Throughout the corpus of their writings, only Mark's Gospel, Second and Third John, Jude and Second Peter were not lucidly attested.

With that in mind, however, the first definitive list, or canon, of the New Testament to be presented was produced in the middle of the second century by the heretic Marcion. Raised in the Christian tradition and son of the bishop of Sinope in Pontus (modern day Turkey), Marcion early on displayed a strong contempt for Judaism and for the material world. By the year AD 144, he left his home and church and journeyed toward Rome where he made a concerted effort to revive Paul and overthrow the teachings of the Old Testament.

Marcion's theological construct was heavily influenced by Gnosticism. Most notably, he agreed with their anti-biblical view in the depravity of the material world and concluded the universe was created by an evil god. Though he freely embraced many aspects of Gnosticism, he rejected the convoluted Gnostic theory of creation and instead proposed a much simpler view. He theorized that there were only two gods: an evil god and a good god. Because of his antipathy for Judaism, he taught Jehovah of the Old Testament must be the inferior and wicked god who created the universe. Besides, he reasoned, Jehovah was a vengeful, vindictive, and capricious deity who punished people unjustly for their actions.

Ruling over the vengeful Jehovah is the compassionate God of the New Testament. This God requires nothing from us; He is merciful and is willing to forgive our iniquities. Salvation is also freely given to everyone since God does not desire to punish humanity but wishes all to come to repentance. Out of his profound love, therefore, God sent his only begotten Son to save all people.

It was only natural, then, that Marcion's dualism led him to reject the Old Testament and seek to promote his views through a misreading of select New Testament writings. So devoted to his overriding theological presuppositions was Marcion that he compiled a list of books he considered to be the true canon. His final list yielded a truncated Gospel of Luke and ten Pauline epistles, which were also similarly expurgated.

Marcion's decision to promote a New Testament listing is telling for this reason. Strong opposition against Marcion's canon bears testimony to the fact that the church already possessed, at least in some rough form, a defined collection of writings which went beyond Marcion's limited canon. Churches functioning throughout the region in which he taught came to be regarded, by other bishoprics, as deviating from established orthodox truths.

Had the majority of believers not already recognized what was authoritative for the church, Marcion's deficient listing might have prevailed. But nowhere do we find evidence of this happening. In fact, the opposite is true. The unanimous consent of the early church Fathers is that they stood united in affirming the authority of the New Testament Gospels and the apostolic writings. Of course, this statement is easily verifiable and finds support throughout the historical record.

During the second half of the second century, Irenaeus, trained under Polycarp, a disciple of the apostle John, quotes from the New Testament on the basis of its authority and provides an apologetic effort as to why the four Gospels are true (and only four). Further, he reckons Acts, First Peter, First John, the Pauline epistles (save Philemon) and Revelation as being equal with the rest of Scripture.

Also during this time period, about AD 170, came the emergence of the *Muratorian Canon*. First discovered in 1740 in the Ambrosian

Library in Milan by a librarian named Muratori, the eighth-century copy of the canon included the four Gospels, Acts, the thirteen letters of Paul, Jude, First and Second John, and Revelation. The manuscript also included a statement that indicated Second Peter remained in dispute since it differed in style from Peter's first epistle. Again, what we discover is that by the late second century, the New Testament canon (the majority text) is confirmed and represented except for a few "Catholic Epistles".

The churches in the East and the West continued to disagree over these final few books. Though sometimes grouped with other Scriptures and generally believed to be beneficial for spiritual nourishment, skepticism prevented their inclusion into the canon for some time until suspicion abated. For example, the West was agnostic toward the book of Hebrews, and Revelation was generally excluded by many in the East until as late as the fourth or fifth century. The Western church remained silent with respect to the books of James, Second Peter, Second and Third John, and Jude until the fourth century and even then were received with skepticism in some circles.

Through a gradual process of recognition, nevertheless, both the Eastern and Western branches of Christendom arrived at a common understanding as to the extent of the canon of the New Testament. The first official document citing the authoritative list of twenty-seven books we have today was promulgated in Athanasius' Easter Letter for the year AD 367. Three decades later at the Council of Carthage, the same twenty-seven books were decreed to be of divine origin and to be read in all the churches.

DETERMINING THE CANON

Sometimes it is alleged that the church determined the extent of the canon through the process of infallible councils, and without the church there would be no canon of Scripture. Such reasoning, however, demonstrates a fundamental misunderstanding of the very nature of the Bible. This point, though mentioned earlier, bears repeating and cannot be overstated. Holy Scripture is an artifact of revelation that came into existence as the by-product of God's inspiration. So when we are discussing the canon of Scripture, what we are really expressing is the extent or limitation of what God has chosen to reveal.

The canon is merely mankind's knowledge of what God has chosen to divulge. Remember, canon is determined by God and exists whether anyone knows it or not. So, for instance, if an individual writes ten books, those books exist whether or not anyone recognizes all ten as being written or not. If, however, the author chooses to reveal his books, then he might do so for a specific purpose, giving insight regarding which books he has authored.

Likewise, once we understand that canon is a special gift given by God for a specific purpose, it becomes all the more clear that God had a purpose in giving us his inspired Word. Believing this will help us to trust that what has been revealed, first through the people of Israel and then through the New Testament church, is truly authoritative and serves a function in his church. God intended to inspire for a specific purpose, so it stands to reason that he did so in order that we might know something about him. In so doing, it does not depend upon any one person or organization, but solely on God who makes himself known.

Understanding canon is from God, in the ultimate sense, is neither a denial that he works through human effort, nor does it contradict the reality that the Spirit leads his people to recognize that which is truly *theopneustos*, God-breathed. In the Old Testament times, he spoke through prophets; in the New, he used apostles to carry his message. Because of this, the early church was able to discern what was truly an artifact of revelation and what was merely useful or even that of dubious origin.

For the early church, the single deciding factor in determining if a book was truly authoritative rested with the conviction that the apostles were legitimately authorized to speak for Christ. An apostle, therefore, or someone directly related or commissioned by one was required. We see examples of this regarding Luke's association with Paul and Mark's relationship with Peter. The development of the canon rested on the knowledge that the Lord commissioned his apostles to speak on his behalf. Both during Jesus' earthly ministry and afterwards, the apostolic message from each of the Twelve remained in concert with the teachings of their Master. Whether in spoken form or written—both of which constituted the same message—the words of the apostles reflected the message and teaching of Christ.

Looking back after the lives of the apostles, the second and third century Christians viewed the apostolic writings as being on equal footing with the Old Testament. Spurious writings inevitably surfaced, with many letters purportedly attributing authorship to an apostle or to some important or influential figure. To mitigate the inadvertent approval of these texts and to counter the so-called apostolic documents, another factor was utilized in determining veracity.

Historically, the process included acceptance and approval in all the churches and not merely usage in isolated communities. The mere acceptance of some writings in remote geographic locations was not sufficient for concluding they were of divine origin. All churches throughout Christendom had to embrace the writings and teach from them. Additionally, epistles claiming apostolic origin had to comport with known orthodoxy. If a book or gospel's message conflicted with accepted teachings in any manner it was rejected (which is why the gospel of Mary and scores of other works were declared spurious soon after they began to circulate). The entirety of a book's message had to bear witness to established truths.

We must also not be quick to forget that the Holy Spirit initially moved upon the authors to write. In so doing, the canon came into existence. Before anyone had the intellectual knowledge of the canon, the canon existed. God foreknew the content and extent—since he was its divine author. As time progressed, the Spirit enlightened believers (the church) of his revelation, leading them in recognizing that which is God-breathed.

Those who still insist Christians are indebted to a particular church organization for recognition of the canon do not fully understand the thrust of the argument, nor do they seem to comprehend the reality that the same Holy Spirit who led men in writing properly guided believers to recognize God's Word. While some find it subjectively comforting to believe they have infallible knowledge of the canon because an infallible magisterium told them so, evangelicals can rightly rejoice with the utmost confidence in knowing the canon of Scripture rests solely on the sovereignty of God and his desire for us to know such things. God is the author of canon, and he has made his Word known to us so that it may instruct us and train us in righteousness so that we may be competent and equipped for every good work (2 Tim 3:16). Just as the believer living fifty years prior to the life of Jesus Christ knew what the Scriptures were and understood them clearly enough to gain salvation apart from any infallible interpreter, the same holds true for the believer today. The crucial point here to understand is the Spirit was working with his chosen people in the Old Testament in helping them to recognize his Word. And the same is true for the New Testament believers. God worked with his elect under the New Covenant in allowing them to discern that which is ultimately God-breathed.

THE RELIABILITY OF THE NEW TESTAMENT

Dan Brown's claim that Constantine and the Council of Nicea fabricated the deity of Christ and made indiscriminate changes to the Bible is unconvincing at best. Not to be outdone, Christians will undoubtedly encounter accusations like the one Brown peddles from a host of skeptics including liberal Christians, Jehovah's Witnesses, Mormons, and Muslims—all of whom attack the veracity and reliability of Scripture for one reason or another. But it's not just opponents of the Bible who question its trustworthiness. Some sincere believers (and others not so sincere) have also expressed doubt that God has preserved his Word in light of the numerous transmissions and translations the documents have been through during the last few centuries. How should the evangelical respond? Understanding the history of biblical transmission, albeit briefly, will serve all believers well in the face of mounting cynicism. Let's briefly consider some of the details.

Without question, the chief line of defense against attacks of corruption of the biblical text lies in the numerical strength of the manuscripts. That is to say, the evidence for the New Testament writings far surpasses that of any other ancient document, bar none. In actuality, if any other classical work had as many copies, its authenticity would never be questioned.

Perhaps what makes the manuscript tradition so compelling is the antiquity of the documents. To date, we possess a dozen New Testament manuscripts dating to within a generation or two of the original documents.[10] The oldest, designated P52,[11] has been dated as early as AD 110, containing portions of John 18—a reality that, for many, once seemed to be a near impossibility. The discovery of the papyrus fragment was, interestingly, invaluable in rebuffing nineteenth-century German scholarship

---

10. P4/P64/P67 (all one manuscript), P32, P46, P52, P66, P75, P77, P87, P90, P98, P104, P108, P109.

11. "P" standing for "papyrus."

which, at one time, insisted that John's Gospel was written in the third century because it contained a high Christology. The once "scholarly consensus," however, was easily dismantled after archeologists uncovered a fragment that was composed only two decades after the original Gospel was penned (provided one accepts a traditional dating).

What is perhaps most stunning—at least to those who deny accuracy in the transmission process—is the degree to which the fragment comports with other manuscripts. The remarkable testimony of P52 is that it reads the same as later manuscripts and codices. Indeed, P52 is just one of numerous fragments that provide early witness to the faithful transmission of the New Testament and helps in recovering the original reading of the text. The more scholars unearth ancient biblical findings, the more empirical evidence is brought forth in defense of textual reliability. With each new discovery, the accuracy of the transmission mission process is only strengthened and confirmed.

Other contributing factors upon which the Christian can rely are the differing text-types and families, the importance of which cannot be overstated. The often-repeated assertion, propounded by Dan Brown and others, of editorial control over the documents of the Bible is without historical warrant. Some radical theories have gone so far as to suggest Constantine ordered the wholesale change of the New Testament during the Council of Nicea.[12] Could such an idea, as far-fetched as it might sound, even be a rational possibility? Even if Constantine wanted to eviscerate the New Testament writings and ordered this implausible endeavor, could it have ever actually been achieved? The simple answer is No. Given that multiple lines of transmission, known as text-types, existed for centuries prior to Constantine, there really is no compelling argument for the possibility of a "Christian Uthman"—someone who gathers all incompatible manuscripts and destroys them *in toto*.[13]

But what exactly is a text-type, and why is it important? A "text-type" or "text-family" refers to the process of grouping manuscripts which share certain common features or readings. Some manuscripts, in fact, might belong to more than one type. Lines of distinction can

---

12. See Brown, Ch. 55.

13. Following the death of Muhammad, there was confusion as to what materials would be included in the Koran. Eventually, the caliphate Uthman (644–656) gave his approbation for an official text and burned all other materials. See Miller, *A Christian's Response to Islam*, 51–53.

oftentimes become blurred, but New Testament scholars have generally agreed upon four text-types in the Bible: Alexandrian, Western, Byzantine, and Caesarean.[14] As is perhaps evident from the names, each text-type received its so-called designation from the geographic location to which it is tied. The importance of understanding this is twofold: one, manuscripts existed in differing regions on multiple continents (to use the idiom *a needle in a haystack* would not even begin to be a proper analogy); and two, even if one family of manuscripts was "corrupted," the other text-types would have been preserved from this insidious reality.

As it was, because the New Testament was written in the common Greek the documents within the first few centuries were able to be transmitted from Jerusalem throughout the Roman Empire and beyond, reaching as far as India. Since the good news was proclaimed to every tribe, tongue, and nation all kinds and classes of people had access to the Word. Even during the apostolic era, believers were able to produce an untold number of copies. Christians—unlike their Jewish predecessors who severely restricted the copying of Old Testament writings—were open about spreading the message of Christ, encouraging their letters to be promulgated to distant lands. Rather than limiting copies to only the wealthy, learned, or scribes, the New Testament was available to anyone for copying. Consequently, the manuscripts were out of the realm of any potential controlling authority or any single person (e.g., Constantine).

Soldiers, traders, slaves, and businessmen all carried the New Testament writings into distant lands even during the generation of the apostles. But because of this freedom to copy manuscripts without distinction, transcription errors were inevitable—which accounts for many of the (minor and insignificant) variations in the extant manuscripts today. Indeed, the overwhelming majority of variations are inconsequential, such as the moveable *nu* (something tantamount to the difference between "who" and "whom"), word order changes, misspellings, omitted words, and so on—but nothing that affects the integrity of the text. What must be kept in mind is that no doctrine of Scripture is grounded upon a variant or disputed reading, because no Christian tenet rests solely upon a single verse.

While many people might view the reality of minor dissimilarities or variant readings in manuscripts as a bad thing, it in fact helps

---

14. For fuller discussion on text-types and families see White, *The King James Only Controversy: Can You Trust the Modern Translations?* 42–48.

in recovering the original text. Because the New Testament books were written over a span of decades and at various locations and were copied and distributed even during the inscripturation process,[15] there was never a period of time in which a singular authority or any group of people could gather all the manuscripts and make substantial emendations or changes to the text. No matter how engrossing it might appear in fiction novels, no person could have possibly inserted the deity of Christ, let alone other essential Christian doctrines. Nor could any one individual, however powerful, assemble all the manuscripts in existence just to harmonize the message of each author. Even if one were to grant the dubious idea of some ruling authority ordering the wholesale change of the New Testament documents the extant manuscripts we have available today, such as P66 and P75, were already buried in the sands of the Egyptian desert long before the convocation of the Council at Nicea in the fourth century.

Beyond easily demonstrating the implausibility of someone changing the entirety of the manuscript tradition (more than 5,000 Greek manuscripts or portions thereof), what is even more remarkable is that when compared to the Byzantine text of a millennium later, for instance, the readings of some ancient manuscripts are nearly identical.[16]

While some might wish God had merely preserved the original documents in order for us to know with certainty the original reading,[17] the reality is one, if he so chooses, can already clearly see the protection and preservation of God's Word. It takes a dispassionate witness to evaluate the evidence in order to reach the same conclusion as the foremost New Testament textual critical scholar Kurt Aland who pointed out several decades ago: "The transmission of the New Testament textual tradition is characterized by an extremely impressive degree of tenacity. Once

---

15. For instance, 1 Tim 5:17–18 reads, "Let the elders who rule well be considered worthy of double honor, especially those who labor in preaching and teaching. For the Scripture says, 'You shall not muzzle an ox when it treads out the grain,' and, 'The laborer deserves his wages.'" Paul is here recognizing two quotations that are "Scripture": one from Luke 10:7 and another from Matthew 10:10.

16. See White, 48.

17. Bart Ehrman asserts that we can never get back to the original reading because we do not have the originals. However, even if we were to find a manuscript that dates to the mid first century, who is to say any humanistic scholar would even accept its authenticity? See White and Ehrman, *Does the Bible Misquote Jesus?*

a reading occurs, it will persist with obstinacy."[18] What this means is that once a variant reading is introduced into a manuscript, it remains—however clearly wrong it might be. That is, an aberrant reading (e.g., clear misspelling, punctuation, and so on) does not simply go away.

If an error was introduced into the manuscript somewhere along the transmission process, it stays. Miscopies, mistranslations, and misspelling are permanent. And how, exactly, is this a good thing? Ensuring errors remain in the text, however blatantly obvious, is beneficial because the present day observer can trust that texts do not merely slip through the cracks or disappear over time, even if only to correct an obvious translation error. Carrying this reasoning to its logical conclusion, then, the tenacity of the text also means that the original reading can be recovered by way of thorough investigations. Given a host of manuscripts that have variant readings, one of them, undoubtedly, is the oldest and original reading.[19]

The illustration has sometimes been used of a jigsaw puzzle. If, for instance, the student begins to reconstruct a 1,000 piece puzzle but has 1,010 pieces in his possession, it is his duty to figure out which 10 pieces do not belong. Knowing that 1,000 of those pieces can correctly make up the original picture, it is his job to find out which 10 pieces are superfluous and do not "fit the puzzle." Similarly, the student of New Testament studies can reasonably demonstrate which minor insertions belong to the category of the extra "10 pieces" and which are part of the original.

One notable example of accurately piecing together the puzzle of the New Testament is illustrated in the example of the longer ending of Mark, namely, Mark 16:9–20. Known as the "longer Marcan ending," this passage naturally flows with the preceding text and comports with other accounts from the Gospels. From a plain reading of the text, there is nothing in the passage itself that would lead one to believe it is dubious, especially in light of other testimonies from Scripture. And yet, as we now know today from textual studies, those few verses were inserted some time after the original was written and distributed. Among the Greek New Testaments produced in recent years all but one include the

---

18. Aland, *The Text of the New Testament*, 291.

19. This is not to say, however, as Aland and others have pointed out, that it is always easily discernable to know what the original reading is. This is oftentimes a difficult and laborious process to distinguish, if even possible, between readings (e.g., Rom 5:1, "we have"; "let us have"). Tenacity, therefore, means we have the original, not that we know with absolute certainty which one is the original.

longer ending in their text, but with qualification. Meaning, all other translations include single or double brackets around the passage, indicating textual variations and explaining verses nine through twenty were a latter insertion.

Be that as it may, this longer ending in Mark's Gospel is found in ninety-nine percent of the extant Greek manuscripts, and it also enjoys a rich tradition. However Codex Vaticanus and Codex Sinaiticus (the oldest major Septuagint manuscripts) end at Mark 16:8, as do a handful of other extant and non-extant manuscripts according to patristic evidence from Eusebius and Jerome.[20] Our understanding of this particular passage is a striking example of tenacity. Even though the majority of Greek manuscripts include the traditional ending, as well as the church incorporating it into her tradition, the original reading was preserved in our oldest codices so that we know today it was not original to Mark's Gospel.

Other ancient voices speaking to the authenticity of the Christian Scriptures must be considered as well. For example, when charges are levied of wholesale changes to the New Testament, rarely, if ever, do skeptics of New Testament reliability consider the patristic sources. Indeed, the early ecclesiastical writers cite New Testament passages quite extensively, so much so, that even if all New Testament sources were eradicated, we could still reconstruct a majority of the content from the early church Fathers alone.[21]

Setting the entirety of the preceding arguments aside for the moment, perhaps the greatest concomitant testimony next to Scripture is the numerous martyrs who sealed the testimony of Christ with their blood. When opponents of Christ's deity contend Jesus was not divine, they must answer the overwhelming number of believers in the first few centuries after Christ who gave their lives with the full assurance they

---

20. See Aland, 291ff. The widespread practice of the Church was eventually superseded by Tradition and the longer ending prevailed. Numerous other manuscripts, even as late as the twelfth century miniscule 304, end with 16:8.

21. Indeed, while the Patristics provide testimony to the reliability, there still remain some problems with their writings. Namely, the Fathers did not always follow a set comprehensive, chapter by chapter listing of verses. Also, they, at times, quoted from memory and not directly from available manuscripts. And finally, it has been documented that some copyists tended to make corrections to the documents. While this undoubtedly provides some, but limited, support for latter emendations, it is nevertheless another line of testimony that must be clearly investigated and thoroughly established that corruption is inherent in all their writings and not merely postulated *a priori*.

were dying for God the Son. One particular example of this confidence is Ignatius, overseer of the church in Antioch, who was sent to Rome because he professed a belief in Christ and taught that Jesus was divine, contrary to Roman law. Writing on his way to the capital, Ignatius recorded these words in AD 110:

> "Now I begin to be a disciple. I care for nothing of visible or invisible things so that I may but win Christ. Let fire and the cross, let the companies of wild beasts, let breaking of bones and tearing of limbs, let the grinding of the whole body, and all the malice of the devil, come upon me; be it so, only may I win Christ Jesus."[22]

Ignatius is only one of many early Christians who faced death without fear. Countless others were sentenced to the flames, to be fed to the lions, or to endure immeasurable suffering and persecution for professing the name of Christ.[23] To postulate that a fourth century council imposed deity upon Jesus is to stand at open variance to the countless testimonies of the saints who gave their lives for a belief in what Christians continue to embrace to this day as orthodoxy.

A FINAL WORD FOR THE EVANGELICAL

It would be easy to continue writing in perpetuity on this subject. This brief overview is far from exhaustive regarding the truths or even the history of the canon. But what we must remember, however, is that the collection of books we possess called the Bible is the complete artifact of divine revelation, sufficient for salvation. In the canon of Scripture, we have the very Word of God. And because of this divine nature and origin, the Bible functions as the sole rule of faith for the church. Until the traditions residing outside of Scripture can be shown to be God-breathed, they do not belong on par with the rest of Scripture.

We can also have confidence that the Bible remains a faithful representation of the original documents, not only from the growing mounds of empirical evidence confirming this statement, but also because of the reality that the canon is ultimately from God. He first moved in history to breathe out his Word, and in so doing, he similarly ensured that his

---

22. Cited in Foxe, *The New Foxe's Books of Martyrs*, 14.

23. For a detailed account of persecutions in the early church, see Eusebius, *The History of the Church*.

Word was preserved. Just as the psalmist declared, "Forever, O LORD, your word is firmly fixed in the heavens" (Ps 119:89).

So the next time you take your Bible in hand, remember its history; recall its origin; but above all, understand that you are holding a true and verifiable facsimile of the Word of God. The words you read on the pages of Scripture are the same words taught and believed by Christians from the earliest generations onward. Therefore, meditate upon its richness, and ponder Gods words day and night. In so doing, you will see the beautiful testimony for which countless men and women throughout the ages have given their lives.

And also do not forget Paul's final exhortation to Timothy shortly before his own death: Continue in the teachings you received since your youth from the Scriptures. For all Scripture is God-breathed and useful for teaching, for reproof, for correction, and for training in righteousness, that the individual of God may be equipped for every good work. Dwelling upon the teachings of Scripture will fully equip the person of God. We should listen, then, to his Word, to his teachings, so that we may grow in grace, in truth, and in knowledge.

Think About It

1. Why is the origin of the Bible important?
2. Why is the Bible the authoritative guide for the church?
3. Why can we trust in the reliability of the Bible as we possess it today?
4. Who determined the canon?
5. In the ultimate sense, how did we get the Bible?

2

Persecution in the Early Church

(64–313)

He knew he would never again see his beloved country and his most cherished friends, nor would he once more set his eyes on the great Temple, or the city of Jerusalem. The thought was too great to fathom. His eyes welled with tears, and he began to weep, not from self-pity but because of the trials and persecution he knew his brothers and sisters in Christ would certainly endure. In fact, he was no stranger to suffering, for on multiple occasions he was beaten with rods, stoned, and even fell victim to multiple assassination attempts for merely proclaiming the good news of Christ Jesus. Now, here he was, sitting in a Roman prison, knowing his impending trial would result in his execution. So he resolved to write one final letter to his most trusted friend in which he would set forth his final words of exhortation.

The apostle Paul—for that was the name of the victim—understood the sobering reality of what it means to be a follower of Christ. He knew intimately what living for Christ entailed. Reflecting upon the numerous persecutions he faced as a believer, he recalled,

> "my persecutions and sufferings that happened to me at Antioch, at Iconium, and at Lystra—which persecutions I endured; yet from them all the Lord rescued me. Indeed, all who desire to live a godly life in Christ Jesus will be persecuted, while evil people and imposters will go on from bad to worse, deceiving and being deceived" (2 Tim 3:11–13).

Paul was not the first to die for the cause of Christ, nor would he be the last. Christian persecution intensified to such an extent in the following century that Tertullian (*c.* 160–225) famously observed, "The blood of the martyrs is the seed of the church." According to the Latin Father of Christianity, without the shedding of blood, the church would not have spread as far, as wide, or as rapidly as it did. Indeed, from its very beginning, the church not only contended with internal dissension from various theological heresies, but she also battled humiliation, condemnation, and persecution from the powerful and mighty Roman Empire.

The Emperor Nero is generally granted the unfavorable distinction of being the first major persecutor of the Christian church beginning in AD 64. But before they faced Nero's imperial maltreatment, Christians encountered conflict from adherents of their mother religion—Judaism. Though believers were not always systematically sought out and victimized, the church, nevertheless, would endure two-and-a-half centuries of physical violence, first by Jews and then from Roman rulers before Constantine converted to Christianity and granted the religion a favorable status.

A NEW JEWISH SECT

It should come as no surprise that Jews who rejected Jesus as the promised Messiah were bound to persecute Christians. During Jesus' earthly ministry, the majority rejected his claims and pursued retribution for the audacious claims of deity. This is clear from the Jewish leaders' continual attempts to entrap Christ from early on in his ministry. From the Jewish perspective, Christianity was a heretical sect within the monotheistic religion.

Attitudes within Judaism toward the Christ-followers varied. Some were apathetic, viewing Christianity as merely another one of the many divergent aspects of the religion. Others, however, took a more rigid and patriotic stance against the new teachings. Still more orthodox believers feared Christians would bring Yahweh's judgment and wrath upon the nation for committing idolatry and blaspheming his name. For these reasons, a number of Jews sought help from the Roman authorities in persecuting the followers of Jesus. For instance, Luke records how the Jews made a united attack against Paul, bringing him before the proconsul, Gallio, in which the Jewish leaders tried to persuade Gallio that the apostle was advocating anarchy and, therefore, a threat to the unity of the empire (Acts 18:12–17). Later on, the apostle is again caught up in the midst of a riot in which he narrowly escapes with his life.

Other biblical examples include the incident when the priests, the captain of the temple, and the Sadducees had Peter and John arrested for teaching that Jesus resurrected from the dead (Acts 4:1–4). Undaunted by the encounter with the Jewish authorities, the apostles continued preaching about Christ. Just a few verses later, we again read of Peter and the other apostles continuing in their efforts to teach the people about the resurrection. The reaction by the Jewish leaders was predictable and, as Luke records, they "were enraged and wanted to kill them" (Acts 5:33). Instead of putting the apostles to death, however, the Jews heeded the advice of Gamaliel and set them free, but not before "they beat them and charged them not to speak in the name of Jesus" (Acts 5:40).

Stephen, though, was not as fortunate. After his encounter with the Jewish leaders where he proclaimed the good news of Jesus Christ, they "were enraged, and they ground their teeth at him" (Acts 7:54). Stephen was dragged out of the city and stoned while a young man named Saul stood by and watched the event unfold. That young man gained tremendous zeal from Stephen's martyrdom, and he subsequently embarked on his own crusade against the early church until his dramatic encounter with the Lord while on his way to Damascus fundamentally transformed his life forever (Acts 9:1–19).

Another striking example of Jewish discord with Christianity is recorded in the Bible and is later confirmed by the Roman historian Suetonius (*c.* 71–*c.* 135). Acts 18:2 indicates, "Claudius had commanded all the Jews to leave Rome." The biblical writer left the story there, while the secular historian provides greater granularity as to why the Jews were expelled. According to Suetonius, he says the Jews were driven from the capital city for their disorderly conduct "because of Chrestus." Most scholars agree this is a clear indication to "Christus," and the Christian's proclamation was causing riots within the city. The fact that the Roman authorities expelled the Jews provides a clear indication that they continued to see the conflict between the two groups as an internal concern within Judaism.

This increasing rift persisted for some until the Roman authorities came to view the Christian religion as distinctly separate from its predecessor—that is, as a *religio illicita*, an illegal religion. So long as the Romans viewed Christianity as a sect of Judaism—which was considered a *religio licita*, a lawful religion—Christians were tolerated, and there was no official imperial persecution throughout the empire.

However, the distinction between the two groups became clearer as the church received more Gentiles, and the Jewish population diminished precipitously. Sporadic acts of violence perpetrated against Christians only served to widen the chasm and did little to help ameliorate the growing tension.

The early church historian Eusebius of Caesarea recorded many incidences of Jewish persecution toward the early church in his, *The History of the Church*. One particularly striking example of aggression is the account of the martyrdom of James, the Lord's brother. Eusebius writes,

> "So they [the Jews] went up and threw down the Righteous one [from the Temple parapet]. Then they said to each other 'Let us stone James the Righteous', and began to stone him, as in spite of his fall he was still alive. But he turned and knelt, uttering the words: 'I beseech Thee, Lord God and Father, forgive them; they do not know what they are doing.' While they pelted him with stones, one of the descendents of Rechab the son of Rachabim—the priestly family to which Jeremiah, the prophet, bore witness, called out: 'Stop! What are you doing? The Righteous one is praying for you.' Then one of them, a fuller, took the club which he used to beat out the clothes, and brought it down on the head of the Righteous one. Such was his martyrdom. He was buried on the spot, by the sanctuary, and his headstone is still there by the sanctuary. He has proved a true witness to Jews and Gentiles alike that Jesus is the Christ. Immediately after this, Vespasian began to besiege them."[1]

Surging physical violence combined with rising Jewish nationalism gave impetus to increased rebellion against Rome. Christians overtly began separating themselves from the Jews. All of this contributed to a new consciousness among Roman authorities in seeing Christianity as a separate, and thus, illegal religion. This separation from Judaism would prove costly during the next several centuries as countless men, women, and children suffered and died for the cause of Christ—bringing Paul's promise to fruition that all who desire to follow Christ Jesus will be persecuted.

---

1. Eusebius, 60. Ironically, even Jewish historians mark this tragic episode as the beginning of a treacherous Roman persecution against the Jews. Most notably, Josephus does not hesitate is writing about this crime as a major factor in the siege of Jerusalem.

CHRISTIAN MARTYRDOM UNDER NERO

By the time Nero reached the Roman throne in October of 54, no one could have imagined the unspeakable horrors he was destined to commit. Nor would anyone have believed the terror and madness that would be associated with his very name. Indeed, even today many Christians are convinced the thirteenth chapter of Revelation contains a riddle that is a specific numerical reference to Nero as the beast (The number 666 signifies the Hebrew form of Nero's name, *Neron Kaesar*). Be that as it may, Nero started his reign as a reasonable leader. At first he was popular, garnering support from the Roman populace. Like any good politician who seeks to gain approbation from the dispossessed, his laws favored the lower classes, and he was able to achieve the popularity he desired, albeit only temporarily. Eventually, however, his lust for grandeur increased and any sensibility or moderation evaporated. His penchant for bloodlust and tyranny are lucidly demonstrated in the executions of his own mother and stepbrother and his irrational hatred of Christians.

After Nero ruled for a decade, the people, including the sophisticated and elite, began to despise their ruler. Rumors circulated of Nero dressing in the skins of wild beasts, roaming the streets of the capital, committing other random and bizarre acts. By the summer of 64, the general consensus was that the emperor was mad.

Such was the state of affairs in the capital when, during a June evening, fires suddenly broke out in Rome. For a week's duration, fires ravaged the capital city. Ten of the fourteen city sections were destroyed. Allegations swirled throughout the city that Nero intentionally ordered the fires so that he could rebuild the city according to his fancy. More and more people started to believe an account which claimed the emperor watched the fire from his palace while dressed as an actor, playing his harp and singing about the destruction of Troy. When Nero discovered the people suspected him of ordering the inferno, he took radical steps in blaming others to allay the suspicions about his own involvement. The Roman historian Tacitus (c. 60–c. 120) records the general belief that Nero ordered the fires and unjustly blamed the Christians:

> "But all the endeavors of men, all the emperor's largesse and the propitiations of the gods, did not suffice to allay the scandal or banish the belief that the fire had been ordered. And so, to get rid of this rumor, Nero set up as the culprits and punished with the utmost refinement of cruelty a class hated for their abomina-

tions, who are commonly called Christians . . . Accordingly, arrest was first made on those who confessed [sc. *to being Christians*]; then, on their evidence, an immense multitude was convicted, not so much on the charge of arson as because of hatred of the human race. Besides being put to death they were made to serve as objects of amusement; they were clad in the hides of beasts and torn to death by dogs; others were crucified, others set on fire to illuminate the night when daylight failed . . . All this gave rise to a feeling of pity, even towards men whose guilt merited the most exemplary punishment; for it was felt that they were being destroyed not for the public good but to gratify the cruelty of an individual."[2]

The pagan historian's record is of tremendous value, for it provides one of the earliest examples of Roman attitudes toward early believers. Tacitus makes it expressly clear that the people believed Nero ordered the fires and unfairly blamed the Christians. But he then seemingly proceeds to justify the hostility, describing how the followers of "Christus" were condemned for their "abominations" and "hatred of the human race." Tacitus is not altogether clear what precisely he means by recording these words, but other second century authors provide a more detailed picture as to why Christians were singled out with a special disdain among the numerous other religions practiced throughout the empire.

The denizens of the empire had their own reasons for despising Christians. Oftentimes, their livelihoods would be threatened by the exclusivity of the Christian message. Christian monotheism, by its very definition, precluded the possibility of any other number of the acceptable gods worshipped in the empire. Priests, merchants, artificers, and others derived income through the sale and practice of idolatry. After Christians introduced their new-found ideas, however, the purchase of idols, contact with dead spirits, and use of sorcerers waned abruptly. Indeed, local commerce was oftentimes disrupted and unable to sustain business after the Christian message took root. Passions flared as a result of perceived interference with their trade, leading the more zealous individuals to commit random acts of violence against believers.

The authorities, likewise, took notice when the multitudes became unruly. Political stability was essential for the unity of such a vast empire. Anything remotely perceived to be a threat to its internal structure was suppressed. So among the groups of misunderstood individuals who seemingly threatened the hegemony of the empire were the Christians.

2. Bettenson & Maunder, *Documents*, 1–2.

Christians were accused of a number of violations including atheism, cannibalism, and incest among other misunderstandings of Christian doctrine and practice.

The charge of atheism should sound peculiar to anyone familiar with Christianity, but the reason behind the accusation was that Christians frequently abstained from superstitious activity and kept from publicly worshipping other gods. For so doing, and for serving an invisible God, Christians were accused of atheism. But not only were the authorities perplexed by the Christians refusal to worship acceptable gods, they also misunderstood the nature of the secret meetings in which believers purportedly "ate and drank the blood of Christ." It was only natural, then, for the Romans to conclude Christians were engaging in cannibalism. After all, apart from understanding the Christian context of a symbolic ceremony commemorating the death of Christ, what else could such language actually mean? Moreover, the "love feasts" in which "brothers and sisters in Christ" greeted each other with holy kisses (cf. Rom 16:16; 2 Cor 13:12) stirred the imagination and led the more curious to speculate about all sorts of hedonistic practices.

All of this, combined with their refusal to offer incense during emperor worship, only deepened the chasm between the authorities and the struggling minority. And, of course, it further perpetuated grave misunderstandings.

The final charge Tacitus addresses concerning "hating humankind" speaks more to the Christians' refusal to participate in the daily activities of the capital than anything else. Social events including the theatre, sports, serving in the army, and the like were so enmeshed with pagan rituals and worship that Christians felt compelled to abstain altogether. This refusal was noticed by the authorities (and Tacitus) who viewed believers with a keen suspicion and feared they would incite rebellion against the rule of law.

Because of these reasons, as the ancient writers inform us, Nero issued an edict against Christians. Many early believers, consequently, were sporadically sought out and martyred, including the two most famous during the Neronian reign, Peter and Paul. While the majority of persecution was more than likely restricted to the capital during Nero's reign, danger in the early church soon grew exponentially worse with only brief periods of respite.

In the year 68, Nero committed suicide after a rebellion had been successful in deposing the tyrannical emperor. Persecution against the church abated, but the laws enacted by Nero remained in place. Several differing rulers gained control over the course of the next two years and the church, by and large, was generally ignored during that period. The season of amnesty, though, was not ordained to last.

PERSECUTION AND MARTYRDOM CONTINUE

Domitian (51–96) is another emperor who holds the dubious distinction for persecuting the Christians. Tertullian wrote of him that he "almost equaled Nero in cruelty,"[3] and Eusebius recorded that,

> "Many were the victims of Domitian's appalling cruelty . . . great numbers of men . . . [were] banished from the country and their property confiscated. Finally, he showed himself the successor of Nero in enmity and hostility to God. He was, in fact, the second to organize persecution against us . . ."[4]

Why some emperors chose to crusade against the Christians while others tended to ignore them is not always clear. In Domitian's case the answer might very well reside in the fact that he was a traditionalist. He loved and respected Roman tradition and wanted to restore the gods and way of life of the ancients. The fulfillment of his dream, therefore, should be considered one of the chief causes of his zealous persecution against Christians.

Also during this period of time in the province of Asia Minor, interestingly, the apostle John was banished to the island of Patmos where he penned the Revelation.[5] But persecution was not only limited to influential leaders and figures within the church. Scores of thousands throughout the rest of Asia Minor were exiled, tortured, or even killed. So in the midst of such great suffering, it is understandable to see why the apostle wrote in such graphic terms when describing imperial Rome. John's language, indeed, displays a far more negative demeanor than the message contained in other epistles or letters. When he speaks of the capital he does

---

3. Eusebius, 82.
4. Ibid., 80.
5. This, of course, supposes a traditional dating of the book of Revelation, which has recently been in contention through modern scholarship. For a scholar's argument advocating a pre-A.D. 70 dating, see Gentry, *Before Jerusalem Fell: Dating the Book of Revelation*.

so in terms of the city rulers being "the great prostitute . . . drunk with the blood of the saints, the blood of the martyrs of Jesus" (Rev 17:1, 6). John could write these sentiments in the context of Rome perpetrating a host of abominable atrocities against him and countless other believers.

Fortunately for the Christians, the widespread and heightened persecution marked the decline of Domitian's reign. Much like Nero during his final years, Domitian was seen as a tyrant, and his list of enemies was quite extensive. So hated was he by the people that his political foes assassinated him in his own palace. Wishing to eradicate the name and memory of the diabolical ruler, the Roman senate subsequently decreed to erase his name from memory, beginning with the removal of his name from every inscription.

The positive aspect to Domitian's death for the Christians was that it provided for them a period of respite. They were, at least for a while, truly a forgotten minority. Nobody in high office seemed to pay Christians much attention, granting them several years of relative peace.

SECOND CENTURY PERSECUTION OF THE CHURCH

Among the best attested and most detailed accounts of Christian persecution in the early years are the records of the "acts of the martyrs" of the second century. Many of these stories provide great specificity and purport to be taken directly from court documents. Further glimpses into attitudes towards Christians during the second century are found in the correspondence between the emperor Trajan (53–117) and Pliny the Younger (*c*. 61–*c*. 112), governor of Bithynia (modern day Turkey).

By the time the governor was appointed to his position, Christianity had spread throughout the Roman province. Pliny indicated there were so many believers in his territory that the pagan temples were nearly deserted and image makers could scarcely sell their wares. The governor knew Christianity was an illegal religion and wrote to the emperor about his troubling dilemma. The Christians "assemble before daylight," he reported, and recite by turns a form of words to Christ "as to a god." More than this, they make vows with each not to commit adultery, theft, or any other such sins. Christians were truly seen as a peculiar group to Pliny, but they were still, nevertheless, outlaws and must be punished accordingly. But any Christian who renounced his faith was spared the consequences of disobeying Roman law.

Any Christian believer brought before Pliny who chose to comply with his demands to denounce faith in Christ was then required to prove their apostasy. Pliny insisted on three compulsory acts to prove the seriousness of the individual. That is, each apostate had to pray to the Roman gods, burn incense to the emperor, and curse Christ—three acts which he believed no genuine Christian would do. If individuals would perform these three acts, he would set them free. However, those who initially refused to comply were given two additional chances to recant of their obstinacy. Those who remained impenitent toward the governor's demands were put to death. In his eyes, this course of action was reasonable, because, after all, he gave his subjects three chances to recant before consigning them to death.

Seeing himself a fair and just man, he endeavored to find out more of this Christian religion—something beyond the sheer obstinacy that so many followers manifested when confronted with imperial edicts. Accordingly, two female Christian slave-girls who were deaconesses in the church were arrested for violating Roman law and were tortured, but the end result was not what he envisioned. Instead, the information provided by the girls only revealed to Pliny what he already knew about the religion. All he uncovered was, in his words, a "perverse and extravagant superstition."

The emperor's response to Pliny was clear. In Trajan's mind, Christians represented a dangerous association to the unity of the empire, and as such, must be punished for their beliefs. However, while fulfilling Trajan's policy of capital punishment, Pliny decreed that Christians are not to be sought out and persecuted but must be dealt with if caught.

What was the Christian response to this sort of policy? The overwhelming majority, with few exceptions, stood noble in the face of persecution. Men and women of all classes and walks of life, learned noblemen and bishops, uneducated peasants and slaves, and innocent children approached torture like their Master. With a confident resolve, they suffered for God. Tertullian tauntingly wrote to the pagan rulers, urging them to continue in their persecutions because that only served to increase the number of converts to Christianity. And he was correct. During the early years of the second century persecution was increasingly seen as a badge of honor.

Believers who cheerfully confessed Christ and stood firm in the face of peril—but were not executed—were given the title of "confessor." Others were honored as "martyrs" or "blood-witnesses" for enduring the pains of affliction and dying as a result. What started out just a few decades earlier with believers meeting in secret to avoid persecution evolved, for a growing number of Christians, into overt fanaticism for wanting to obtain martyrdom. Hoping to be offered up in a similar manner as Christ and the apostles, many turned themselves into the authorities. Honor on earth was increasingly viewed as the Christian's highest achievement. Tertullian tells the story of a throng of Christians in Ephesus who pleaded with the pagan authorities to execute them. The governor obliged at first, thinking it might prove to be good sport, but after it became obvious the peace in which the Christians died, he refused to execute any more. He sent the rest away calling them "miserable creatures."

This same intense desire to die a martyr's death is, perhaps, most clearly attested in the ultimate fate of Ignatius, the second century bishop of Antioch, who was condemned to die by the Roman authorities. After being captured by the authorities for being a vocal Christian, Ignatius was sent to the capital city to be executed. His martyrdom was to coincide with a celebration that was to take place in Rome. On his journey to the capital city, he wrote seven letters. All have survived and are considered to be some of the most valuable documents for our understanding of the early church.

Legend states that Ignatius, born around AD 30, was the little child whom Jesus placed in the midst of the disciples in response to their "Who is the greatest in the kingdom?" question (Matt 18:1–4). While the tale will presumably never be verified as authentically true, the bishop of Antioch was undoubtedly an influential leader in the Christian community, serving in one of the most famous churches. His stature and popularity grew to such a staggering degree that he was eventually afforded the title "the bearer of God."

History has failed to preserve the details surrounding the arrest and trial of Ignatius, or the events that precipitated the accusations against him. What is known from his letters is that there were several opposing factions within the church at Antioch. Ignatius opposed some who were teaching heretical doctrines. It is unclear what precisely those aberrant teachings were or who exactly he condemned, but for one reason or another, he was arrested, tried, and ordered to Rome to be executed.

Along the way to the imperial city, he was met by a number of Christians who desired to catch a glimpse of the famous bishop. Since no general persecution was being waged against Christians at the time (only those who were accused were guilty of "crimes"), he was able to be greeted by other bishops, friends, and well-wishers. In total, the bishop wrote seven letters to churches, offering words of encouragement and hope. But arguably the most significant letter of the seven was his letter addressed to the church in Rome.

Rumors had reached Ignatius that the Christian leaders in Rome were attempting to free him from captivity. Discovering this plot distressed the bishop greatly. The possibility of losing his martyr's crown was devastating, so he wrote to the church accordingly: "I fear your kindness, which may harm me. You may be able to achieve what you plan. But if you pay no heed to my request it will be very difficult for me to attain unto God."[6] Ignatius goes on to explain his chief purpose and motivation is to suffer the same fate as his Master. He asks for prayers, not to be freed from bondage, but for the strength and perseverance to endure the pains of persecution. The Christians in Rome complied with his request. In the end, Ignatius received the very thing for which he sought—to suffer and to be free in Jesus Christ. The bishop was only one of many whose blood was spilled by the "great prostitute," Rome.

PERSECUTION IN LATER CENTURIES

At the dawn of the third century there was still no widespread policy of persecution against Christians, despite some local and sporadic harassment. That is to say, even though Trajan's anti-Christian policies remained in place, the church was not yet confronted with any other overt policies that deeply affected its members. That reality, however, would soon change. The third century marked widespread imperial maltreatment and culminated in the great persecution of the late third century. It would not be until Constantine defeated his political rivalry at the Milvian Bridge that persecution finally abated. In all, the three emperors who would prove most pernicious to the church were Septimius Severus (193–211), Decius (249–251), and Diocletian (284–305).

Each emperor had his own reason for persecuting the Christians. In the case of Septimius Severus, he was convinced the supreme deity was the *Sol Invictus*, Unconquered Sun. Because of his beliefs, the emperor proposed new legislation indicating all gods were permissible so long as every individual acknowledged the Sun as the greatest of all gods.

---

6. Gonzalez, *The Story of Christianity: The Early Church to the Dawn of the Reformation*, 43.

Needless to say, persecution against the seemingly obstinate Christians only increased due to this policy. The year of his edict was 202, and it was during this time period that such notable Christians as Irenaeus and the father of Origen suffered martyrdom for failing to acknowledge the Unconquered Sun.

Also during this troubling time in church history are the famous martyrdoms of Perpetua and Felicitas. Both women were charged, not with being Christians *per se*, but with willfully disobeying the imperial edict and converting recently to Christianity. The heroine of the ancient account *Martyrdom of Saints Perpetua and Felicitas*, a work probably from the pen of Tertullian, is Perpetua (*c.* 181–203), a wealthy woman who inspired devotion and loyalty from her slaves and friends, even to the point of death. When Perpetua and her companions were arrested, her father pleaded with her to repudiate the name of Christ in order to spare her life. She refused, answering simply that abandoning her faith was not an option. She was a Christian, and this reality could not be altered.

Perpetua was pregnant at the time of her arrest, and so she prayed that her life would be spared because of this. The trial dragged on for several months and, during the course of that entire affair, she gave birth to a daughter while still imprisoned in a jail cell alongside her personal slave and sister in Christ, Felicitas. Concerned for her at the sight of her reaction to the intense pain in labor and delivery, the jailor asked how she expected to face death courageously when she moaned so greatly in childbirth. Undaunted, she replied that when she encounters the beasts, she will be suffering for Christ. But before that fateful day arrived, she encountered more afflictions. The hardest ordeal she faced was the adoption of her child. Seeing that she had no other option, she begrudgingly gave away her baby to another Christian woman so that her daughter would be raised in the household of believers. Believing that someday she would be reunited in heaven with her baby girl, the hope she possessed gave her the resolve to conquer her fears and to face death courageously.

When the day of their scheduled martyrdoms arrived, Perpetua and Felicitas were not the first to die. Three other Christians were first dragged into the arena for the spectators' amusement. Wild beasts greeted the anxious men, only to attack and kill the first two victims but curiously refused to touch the third. After the soldiers unsuccessfully bated the animals to attack the man, the soldiers were compelled to ram through the man with their swords. Perpetua and Felicitas were next brought into the arena where they were to be gored by a seething bull. Once inside, it did not take long for the bull to attack. After the initial assault, Perpetua was the first to be thrown to the ground. She stood, regained her composure as much as practical under the given circumstances, and asked her servant to fix her hair. Loose hair was a sign of mourning, and she did not want anyone in the crowd to think she was grieving. For her, it was a joyous day. She was only moments away from entering into eternity to spend with her Savior. Nothing could be more joyous. Despite the best efforts of the animal, the bull failed to achieve its intended purpose. Both blooded and bruised from being rammed repeatedly by the charging animal, the two women kissed each other goodbye before finally dying at the hand of Roman soldiers.

Stories such as those of Perpetua and Felicitas rapidly circulated, and the popularity of Christianity only seemed to increase. The Christian message was infectious. Nothing the authorities employed could stop its spread, though many tried. Then, a later emperor, Decius, implemented a new tactic. He reasoned martyrdom only increased the numbers of the church, as Tertullian openly boasted, so he did not desire to make any more martyrs. Instead, his goal was to create apostates. Surely, he reasoned, if enough pain was inflicted upon Christians without the benefit of dying for their cause, they would be more inclined to renounce their faith. So Decius enacted his machinations in the hope that the spirit of Christians would be obliterated once and for all.

Thus, Christians in the mid-second century found themselves faced with a new challenge. Relatively few Christians were martyred during Decius' reign since his goal was to make apostates and to restore the pagan religions of previous generations. Torture and imprisonment were the norm throughout the empire. So instead of local and sporadic persecution resulting in death, the universal policy of the authorities was a systematic approach to force believers into repudiating their faith. Fortunately for Christians, though, Decius' time in power was brief. After reigning for two years, Gallus succeeded Decius as emperor in 251 and set aside his policy of persecution. The church was once again spared of pernicious Roman policy for a few decades until the assaults resumed and ultimately reached the zenith during the reign of Diocletian.

Like previous emperors, Diocletian had his own personal reason for attacking Christians. He did not begin his reign with hatred toward followers of Christ; it was a junior emperor who persuaded him otherwise.

At the start of his reign, Diocletian had instituted some organizational changes. Part of this reorganization included dividing the empire into two sections with four emperors ruling: an "augustus" ruling in the East with a junior emperor ("caesar") and a second "augustus" serving in the West, also having a junior emperor ("caesar") under him. Included in this new structure was a line of succession in which the caesar would eventually be promoted to augustus. Diocletian hoped this new command structure would prevent the outbreak of future civil wars—wars that were becoming inherent within the empire.

As it turned out, one of the junior emperor, Galerius, noticed a general disapproval of military service by Christians. In fact, he found Christians' refusal to join the army troubling and saw it as potentially dangerous to the stability of the empire. Eventually he was able to persuade Diocletian to expel any Christians currently serving in the military and ultimately convinced the ruling emperor to issue a new edict against them. So in 303 Diocletian instituted his new policy that removed Christians from any position of responsibility within the empire, confiscated property, and ordered all Christian documents to be destroyed, including the Scriptures.

In the wake of this new wave of terror, a fire broke out in the imperial palace. Just as had happened in Nero's day, the emperor—who some say started the fire himself—was quick to cast blame on the Christians. Violence against believers subsequently increased, and what ensued were some of the most egregious and flagrant acts.

The sight of human suffering only seemed to fuel the emperor's zeal for brutality. Some of the most horrific events were committed at Diocletian's instigation. Preserved in the writings of Eusebius are some detailed accounts of Christians being bound in red-hot irons while "the smell of burning flesh rose to the heavens;" of others having their flesh stripped to the bone with shells or iron hooks; of women given to gladiators and soldiers who satisfied insatiable lusts; of people having eyes scooped from the sockets; of bodies burning in flames; and other appalling tortures conceived of by only the most depraved minds. Yet, in the midst of these horrific and unimaginable sufferings, many Christians could have escaped the pain with a single word. Amazingly, though, many gallantly refused to recant and instead endured suffering for the promise of a greater future.

Periods of misery continued sporadically throughout the next several decades until a young emperor, through political maneuvering and military victory, defeated the emperor in the West at the battle of the Milvian Bridge. It was at that spot that Constantine, on the eve of the battle, had a revelation in which he was told to place a Christian symbol on the shields of his soldiers. The emperor complied and was, by a stroke of good fortune, victorious the next day. Constantine viewed his decisive win as proof that the God of Christianity was indeed the one true God. More than this, though, the victory gave Constantine control of the Western half of the empire, while the East was still under the control of Licinius.

The two rulers allied and agreed that persecution to Christians should cease and came to a compromise which stated churches, cemeteries, and personal property would be restored to the Christians. This agreement signed in 313 is generally known by its formal title, the "Edict of Milan."

Signing the edict ushered in a new wave of prosperity. Christianity was no longer treated as a *religio illicita*. With Constantine's conversion to the monotheistic religion, he gave the Christian faith a status it had never before achieved in the empire. Though Christianity would never officially become the religion of the empire during his lifetime, he paved the way for Christians to receive favorable treatment from future generations. His protection facilitated the refinement of doctrine and ensured the growth and expansion of a religion which the greatest empire in history only a few years earlier had attempted to eradicate but was unsuccessful in so doing. Indeed, even the gates of hades could not, and did not, prevail against the church.

THE FATE OF CHRISTIANS

When Jesus warned his followers, "If they persecuted me, they will persecute you" (John 15:20), he was foretelling the inevitable consequence believers will encounter. Even the pagan Roman historian, Tacitus, spoke of the "immense multitude" of Christians who were murdered in Rome. The catacombs in that city and stretching for nearly nine-hundred miles are said to contain the bones of some seven million martyrs according to the nineteenth-century calculations of two noted historians.[7] Whatever

---

7. Schaff, *History of the Christian Church*, 2:40.

the actual number, it does not diminish the reality that the early Christian church was methodically sought out for destruction because of so-called "civil crimes". The great sufferings are primarily the reason the ante-Nicene age is held in reverence and gratitude. The church owes much to the many men and women who suffered and perished for Christ Jesus.

It is hard for most Christians today to fathom persecution, let alone suffering martyrdom for a cause. However, if believers truly trust God and rely upon his Word, they should not be surprised to discover the reality of facing trials and persecution. Every professing believer must be ready, as Paul warned, to suffer for the name of Christ.

The only way to ensure that Christians are equipped to that end is to heed the words of the apostle as he wrote his final exhortation to Timothy. "Continue in what you have learned and have firmly believed, knowing from whom you learned it and how from childhood you have been acquainted with the sacred writings, which are able to make you wise for salvation through faith in Christ Jesus" (2 Tim 3:14–15). There is only one way to be acquainted with the Bible and that is to mediate upon the Word continually. If professing Christians do not care to be in the Word, how can they expect to suffer for the Word?

Persecution is the fate of believers, although not all are called to martyrdom. Persecution exists in various forms and degrees. What we must consider is if we are willing to follow in the footsteps of the confessors and martyrs or if we would instead choose the easy course of the apostates. Every day God's people encounter choices in which we must decide if we are going to follow Christ or chase after the world? Remember those who have gone before you, and consider what they sacrificed for the Lord. The question every believer must ask is: "Am I willing to do the same for the Lord if called to suffer for his name?"

Think About It

1. What does the Bible say about Christians and persecution?
2. Why does God allow persecution?
3. What role did persecution play in the development of the church?
4. Have you ever been persecuted for your beliefs? How did you respond? What would you do differently?
5. What are some benefits of persecution?

3

The Arian Controversy

(318–381)

From the earliest moments, Christianity has been rife with theological controversies. During the life of the apostles, the Jerusalem church contended over the issue of circumcision; Paul wrote voluminously against the Judaizers in the Galatian church; and John contended with proto-Gnosticism. And this was all within the lifetime of Jesus' own immediate followers. The second century after Christ proved to be no different. Gnosticism came to the forefront of the apologetic efforts in discourse and debates. By the third century, the central focus was on the restoration of professing believers who denied the faith in the face of persecution. At the dawn of the fourth century, these controversies were no longer a serious threat to the universal church, though there remained small pockets of bitter dissenters. Yet, in each of these cases, the victor appealed to Scripture and a clear reasoning from the Word in order to win the day.

Up to this point, the civil authorities had restrained themselves from intervening in any theological quibbling. The controversies within the church remained there and were resolved through internal introspection. The church had no desire to turn to the civil authorities to resolve ecclesiastical disputes, but things were soon to change.

With the conversion of Constantine to Christianity in 312 and his rule over the empire, the likelihood of civil interference in theological schisms was more than a mere possibility—it became certain. The unity of the Christian church was foundational to the cohesion of the empire. For this reason, Constantine became concerned when he discovered a bishop and a presbyter from Alexandria in North Africa were disputing over the nature of Christ. Fearing possible disruption to his civil structure, Constantine called together bishops throughout the empire in 325 to settle the matter once and for all (or at least that was his desired result).

What followed, however, was imperial intervention and political persuasion that made the Arian controversy fester well after the council decreed its canons. Nevertheless, what clearly became evident was God's involvement in ensuring the truths of his Word were secured for ages to come.

BACKGROUND OF THE CONTROVERSY

To gain the proper perspective of the Arian controversy, it must be remembered that Arianism's root are to be found in the centuries prior to the time of Constantine. Indeed, the controversy found impetus through the teachings and doctrines of earlier Christians and their views concerning the nature of God, namely, Justin, Clement of Alexandria, and Origen (among others). In attempting to prove the rationality of God, Christian apologists of the late first and early second century—many of whom were influenced by Greek thought—appealed to pagan philosophers and sages for their use of wisdom and reason.

One practical problem with this approach was that it demonstrated an over-reliance upon human ability to reason. Instead of relying upon the Holy Spirit to guide unbelievers into truth, the early apologists turned to (or were at least greatly influenced by) Plato, Aristotle, Plotinus, and others when reading and interpreting the writings of sacred Scripture. In so doing, these early Christians attempted to bridge the gap between the Greek philosophical ideas of a supreme being, the afterlife, and sinful actions by pointing out the close connection between the Greek's previously held beliefs and Christian teachings. The danger in this pursuit was a heavy emphasis on allegorizing the Scriptures and a form of syncretism, that is, taking various pieces from differing systems and molding them into Christian thought in order to make Christianity more palatable to unbelievers (as was the case with Gnosticism, which will be discussed later).

So with this Greek philosophical influence in mind, the third century believer, Origen (c. 185–254), a teacher from Alexandria and arguably the greatest theological mind in the church during his time, provides a clear historical background for the controversy. The roots of

Arianism can be seen in Origen's contradictory Christological teachings. Correctly attributing attributes of deity to Christ, he found favor with orthodox doctrine on the notion and identity of Christ's *substance*. Where he strayed and found himself at odds with orthodoxy was in his zeal for distinction and separateness between the Father and the Son. In this manner, Origen was led to the inevitable conclusion, stemming from his presuppositions, that the latter was subordinate to the former. That is, he taught a clear subordination of the Son and concluded that Christ was in some manner beneath the Father—though he at times referred to the Son as the *Theos Deuteros*, the second God. To what extent Christ was subordinate and what precisely he meant by his conclusions is unclear.

What is known, however, is that Arius (*c.* 256–336), a presbyter in Alexandria, took Origen's view of the relationship between the Father and Son and carried it a step further. Arius concluded that if the Son is of a different *substance* than the Father, it is only reasonable to assert the Son is a created being. Arius, overstating the Origenistic view of subordination, taught that while Christ was, without question, the creator of the world, he was, nevertheless, still a created being (unlike the Father) and was, therefore, not truly divine.

To buttress his position, the Alexandrian presbyter appealed to passages such as John 14:28 where Jesus said, "I am going to the Father, for the Father is greater than I." Elsewhere, Christ seemed to demonstrate limited knowledge of future events (Mark 13:32), was in subjection to the Father (1 Cor 15:28), and unable to accomplish anything of his own accord (John 5:19). For Arius, these passages provided biblical credence to the doctrine of subordinationism. What Arius seemingly rejected or failed to comprehend was the biblical concept of the Son willingly emptying himself (Phil 2:7) in order to take on the form of man. He did this of his own free accord, not being obliged or compelled to do so by the Father. However, during his incarnation, Jesus was still fully divine, having all the attributes of deity yet choosing not to access them. In so doing, then, his human nature was limited, which is what we read of in certain passages. Arius, though, made some aberrant conclusions from over-relying upon these "humanity" passages, much to the exclusion and misunderstanding of the entirety of the biblical doctrine.

Moreover, if the Son was begotten by God, he rationalized, it stands to reason that there was a time when the Son was not.[1] Yes, Arius believed Christ was the first and greatest of all beings, but Jesus was, nevertheless, created at some point. God then adopted this chief being as his Son, and thus the Son is worthy of worship because of God's exulted status bestowed upon Christ.

So when the well-liked Arius began teaching in 318 in opposition to Alexander's position that the Son of God had existed eternally, being "generated" eternally by the Father, he was promptly condemned by the ecclesiastical rulers. Unmoved by Alexander's condemnation and opposition from other churches, a local council convened in 321 and declared Arius a heretic. But the matter was not settled there.

Arius moved to Palestine where he continued to promote his aberrant views of the relationship between the Father and the Son. Once Alexander discovered where Arius was operating, he began a letter writing campaign, accusing him of perverse teachings and warning the churches against those he called *Exukontians*, from a phrase in Greek meaning "out of nothing." Arius, however, was well received by some and gained a favorable status with the people. Over the course of the next few years, the matter continued to fester until it caught the attention of the Emperor Constantine.

To the modern reader, Arius' conclusion might appear untenable, but it would have seemed quite reasonable for the believer who, living in the fourth century, was inculcated with pagan philosophy. Before the time of Arius, Gnosticism spread like wildfire, even influencing the thinking of some Christians (as evidenced by the numerous warnings in the New Testament against an early form of Gnosticism). While the Gnostic movement is not always easily definable—since there is no singular connected tradition—there are, nevertheless, some commonalities that distinguish Gnosticism from other viewpoints.

Gnostics, generally speaking, believed the material world was essentially evil. So for some influenced by this way of thinking, it seemed logical to conclude God could not have come in the form of man. To do so would be to admit God was essentially evil. Arius' adoptionist view,

---

1. The Greek term *monogenes*, sometimes translated into the English as "begotten," has created difficulties in understanding. The term literally means "unique" or "one of a kind". In this light, when *monogenes* is applied to Christ, it is a way of subscribing preeminence to the Son and not merely turning Jesus into a creation.

consequently, permitted Christians to embrace the Son as a supreme being while still maintaining a transcendent view that God alone is holy and pure. Making Christ subservient to God fit the worldview of many and squared with the pagan philosophy.

But even with so many non-Christian worldviews permeating much of society and thought, the faithful within the church recognized the pernicious consequences that would naturally follow from Arius' aberrant beliefs. When Arius introduced his viewpoint, the single most important tenet of the Christian religion was under assault—the deity of Christ. To deny the equality of the Son with the Father is to deny the Trinity. Without affirming three coequal and coeternal persons, namely, the Father, the Son, and the Holy Spirit, share the one Being that is God, the biblical doctrine of the Trinity necessary crumbles. Alexander, Athanasius, and every other orthodox believer alive during the early fourth century could not hold the Scriptures in their hands and deny the trinitarian doctrine. They believed in the Trinity, not because the external church or some ecumenical council told them so, but because the Bible, when taken in its completeness, teaches these divine truths.

Additionally, the subordination of Jesus to the Father also calls into question the validity of worshipping Jesus. After all, God expressly forbade any foreign worship: "You shall have no other gods before me" (Exod 20:3). If Arius was correct, Christians wrongly impute deity to Jesus and consequently blaspheme God and, by so doing, violate the first commandment daily. If Christ is lesser than the Father then Christians are guilty of idolatry. For these reasons, orthodox believers rejected the inferior view of Jesus of which Arius taught, though not all were convinced.

The prevalent pagan philosophy of Arius' day, combined with his oratorical skills and power of persuasion, resulted in the growing acceptance of his anti-trinitarian teachings. Alexander (d. 326), the bishop of Alexandria (and later Athanasius who became bishop after Alexander's death), understood the profound implications of his teachings and clearly apprehended the thrust of the controversy. The reality of redemption and the perfection of salvation would be utterly null and void if a mere created being (however exulted) was supposed to unite sinful man with Almighty God. The chasm between the two is so great that no one short of God himself could actually mediate between the creature and the Creator. No finite being could do the necessary work required by an infinite God.

The Christian religion is a revelation of the unity of God and mankind through the work of a divine Being. Arius devalued the orthodox teachings by only furthering the gulf between the former and latter. Arianism, whether purposeful or not, denigrated the person of Christ by reducing him to a mere created being; it replaced a divine Redeemer with an elevated demi-god on par with Zeus, Hercules, or any other mythical god.

Few believers thought through the logical ramifications of Arianism the way Alexander and Athanasius did. So it was Alexander who first earnestly took umbrage with Arius, but it would be Athanasius, with his zealous defense of Christological orthodoxy, who is best remembered for standing courageously against the Arian assault.

With Arius' denial of Christ's deity and growing support from other bishops, the Arian controversy was bound for a widespread audience. The issue was destined to come to head, especially in light of the two opposing and incompatible tenets of faith. Both Alexander and Athanasius maintained: (1) Christ and the Holy Spirit are God; (2) both are distinct from one another and also from the Father; and (3) God is still one Being (though in three divine Persons). Arius, by contrast, argued that Christ was of a different *substance* (or being) from the Father since he was, in the final analysis, created by the Father.

When Constantine first heard of the quarrel, he was inclined to leave it as a misunderstanding of words. He wished to settle the matter through diplomatic means and used the bishop Hosius of Cordova to negotiate a truce, but the attempt proved unsuccessful. Hosius' mediatorial efforts failed to arrest the growing tension and after accepting the advice of several bishops, Constantine summoned the first ecumenical council of Christian bishops. The emperor hoped the council would be able to give a final decision once and for all regarding the relationship between Jesus and God.

The stage was set. Three views were to be presented and discussed: the orthodox view, Arianism, and semi-Arianism. Which of the three competing views would rule the day?

MEETING AT NICEA

Two decades into his reign, Constantine had undertaken some radical changes, including moving the capital from Rome to Byzantium (later changed to Constantinople; modern day Istanbul). So by the year 325 when it became evident the Arian controversy could not be ameliorated amicably, the emperor summoned the bishops of the empire to a small town called Nicea outside the new capital city. In total, 318 bishops attended (only seven of which were from the Latin or Western church) to ruminate over some troubling questions, most notably, the deity of Christ and the relationship of the Trinity.[2]

Gathered together were scores of men who, just a few decades prior, endured untold suffering and still wore the scars of persecution. Now, believers openly gathered at Nicea to discuss Christian doctrine without fear of reprisal. Bishops were called at the behest of the emperor for an all-expense paid trip in order to resolve the theological matter peaceably. Yet, from the beginning, the doctrine in question divided the council into three parties: orthodox, Arian, and Semi-Arian (or middle ground).

The orthodox party was, at first, in the minority, but surely not in theological stature or clout. Among the bishops who tenaciously subscribed to the full deity of Christ were the bishop of Rome, the bishop of Jerusalem, Hosius (the court bishop for Constantine), Alexander, and the great juggernaut of orthodoxy, Athanasius (though not a bishop at the time). These are just a few of the many Christians who held to this ancient belief. Indeed, long before the council commenced in Nicea, bishops, presbyters, deacons, and believers throughout the Christian world held to the deity of Christ.

Standing at open variance to the orthodox position were the Arians, led by Eusebius of Nicomedia (not to be confused with Eusebius of Caesarea, the church historian and other Nicene participant). Though small in number, Arius (only a presbyter) and Eusebius were influential in garnering enough support to speak before such an august assembly.

---

2. Ironically, after nearly three centuries of the bishop of Rome supposedly functioning as the Vicar of Christ and the universal head of the church, the bishop was not the one to call the council nor was he present. Instead, he sent two delegates in his stead. What is even more interesting is that there is no historical record of the legates even participating in the proceedings but left the lead roles to men such as Constantine, Hosius of Cordova, Eusebius of Caesarea, and Alexander of Alexandria, among others.

In stating their case, the Arians first proposed a creed which stated, to the effect, Christ, a created being, was the first and greatest of all God's creation, but, nevertheless, was created. "The Son had a beginning, but God is without beginning." To say the proposal did not go over well is to understate the situation badly. In fact, after reading the decree the crowd turned tumultuous and tore the creed to pieces. Because of the violent, negative reaction against the wording, all but two of the original eighteen signers abandoned the cause of Arius.

Seeing this situation and desiring a peaceful solution, the renowned historian, Eusebius of Caesarea, personal friend of the emperor and admirer of Arius, sought a compromise between the two positions. Desiring to mediate a settlement, he presented the council with his own creed that acknowledged the divinity of Christ in generic biblical terms, but avoided the use of the controversial term, *homoousios*, of the same substance. For Eusebius, it was permissible to call Jesus "God," but in so doing, he stressed one should qualify that to mean his substance or essence was only *like* the Father. Eusebius wanted to avoid the term meaning *same*. He clearly distrusted the term *homoousios*, because it was used by earlier heretics who said Jesus and the Father were one person (Modalists). Instead, he preferred the term *homoiousios*, of like substance. In so doing, he hoped to avoid the error of both Arius and Modalism.

The Arians were ready to accept the wording of the new creed (omitting the term *homoousios*, "of the same substance") but their willingness to embrace the wording made the orthodox bishops suspicious. If the Arians could embrace such language in light of their convictions, the "same substance" participants reasoned, the creed surely must not be traditional enough.

The emperor clearly saw Eusebius' compromise would never pass in its current form so he suggested, presumably with the assistance of his bishop, Hosius, the word *homoousios* should be included in the decree. And after some collaboration it was added. Finally, what emerged from that suggestion was the Nicene Creed we have today:

> "I believe in one God the Father Almighty; Maker of heaven and earth . . . And in the Lord Jesus Christ, the only begotten of the Father before all worlds. God of God, Light of light, very God of very God, begotten, not made, being of one substance with the Father."

In the end, all but two attendees signed the creed. The two Egyptian bishops who obstinately refused to sign were subsequently exiled along with Arius. Arius' books were burned, and all who followed him in doctrine were deemed heretics. Thus began the tragic example of theological intolerance, and this instance provides us with the first example of civil punishment for heresy. Before the council, the greatest punishment enacted was excommunication, but after civil interference, banishment and even death were added as forms of sanitizing the church. Indeed, all of this culminated in the use of the sword for political hegemony, something that never fully reached its apex and culminated in one of the darkest periods of the church—the Inquisition of the medieval ages.

REACTION TO ARIANISM

Victory at the Council of Nicea was short lived. Some were convinced that the Nicene party ruled the day because Constantine's influence determined the outcome. After all, it was he who proposed the inclusion of *homoousios*. In so doing, opponents of Athanasius argued the decision rendered by the council was based on political calculation and not on theological conviction. Because of imperial intrusion into the matter, the deity of Christ required several more decades, and much more persuasion, before it took root throughout all Christendom.

Indeed, the debate concerning the nature of Christ was far from settled. Arianism spread through many churches, especially in the East. Constantine's successor was no friend to Nicene orthodoxy either. Under Constantius, council after council was convened to address the Arian issue. Most importantly, though, regional councils meeting in Ariminum, Seleucia, and Sirmium presented Arian and semi-Arian creeds, and numerous leaders were forced into subscribing to them. Even Liberius, the bishop of Rome, defiled the office for a time by embracing the Arian heresy. Hosius was another leading bishop who, being nearly one-hundred years of age, was coerced by imperial threats into publicly accepting Arianism. While it seemed a very real possibility that Arianism would rule the day, there was a lone voice that remained strong for orthodoxy.

Athanasius remained the one vocal proponent of Nicene orthodoxy who refused to capitulate to the overwhelming pressure to disavow his belief that Christ was of the same substance as the Father (along with the Holy Spirit). Holding his position with such tenacity against his many foes, he responded simply when told of everyone else abandoning the cause of orthodoxy: "Athanasius against the world!" And so it seemed. Undaunted from his position, he was driven by force from his see on five separate occasions, but he still persisted in championing the truth. Athanasius was able to stand for Christ's deity in spite of extreme pressure and mounting opposition because of the clear testimony of Scripture. And that is eventually what ruled the day.

Like so many other movements that depend on political prowess, Arianism eventually grew fragmented, and individuals began to disagree among themselves. There was no Athanasius who fought so determinedly to keep the movement strong, and it didn't take long before bickering and fighting caused its downfall. Arianism's influence and stature rapidly waned. By the year 381, a council met in Constantinople to affirm what Nicea asserted and what Athanasius fought so doggedly to uphold—that is, Christ is God. The party that contended from Scripture ultimately ruled the day, and that expression of Christ's nature as defined at Nicea and Constantinople remains the standard of orthodoxy today.

RESPONDING TO ERROR, THEN AND NOW

The entire foundation regarding Christ's nature can be traced to a misunderstanding of biblical text about who he is. The Arians essentially argued: God the Father alone is uncreated. Everything proceeding from him, including his Son, is created, and thus is of a different substance. After all, Christ is described as "the firstborn of all creation" (Col 1:15) and "the beginning of God's creation" (Rev 3:14). So does this not lend biblical support to the Arians in their assumption of Christ being created and thus of a different substance? What is to be done with these verses?

We must keep in mind that the word translated as "firstborn" is *prototokos*, but the Greek could also be translated as "first-bearer." Meaning, Christ is the preeminent One over all creation. This idea is more clearly brought out by the biblical writers in the following verses of those passages in Colossians and Revelation where they make it clear *prototokos* is not dealing with the temporal notion of generation or creation of Christ. Indeed, even if the Greek were to be translated as *firstborn*, this does not necessarily follow or imply that Christ was a created Being. Recall in Genesis that even though Jacob was not the older brother, he still held the position of being the firstborn. Status determines firstborn and not time. Christ, therefore, is the *firstborn*, the preeminent One. This teaching is so well attested in the entirety of Scripture that no one can rightly deny its clear instruction and remain faithful to God's Word.

The doctrine of Christ's deity does not rest on wishful thinking or a few dubious passages. While it is true the Bible nowhere explicitly states that Christ and God share the divine essence, there are multiple passages that plainly and directly affirm Christ's full deity and equality with God (Isa 9:6; John 1:1, 8:58–59, 18:5–6; Rom 1:5; Phil 2:5–7; Col 2:9; Heb 1:8). Other passages strongly affirm Christ's deity either through indirect declarations or attributing aspects of deity to him.

Understanding this, Athanasius and others recognized the importance of the deity of Christ and why it should be embraced over against Arianism. Perhaps Athanasius summed it up best when, speaking about the Arian movement, he wrote these words: "Nor does Scripture afford them any pretext; for it has been often shown, and it shall be shown now, that their doctrine is alien to the divine oracles."[3]

Contained within this single sentence we have a glimpse into the authority espoused by Athanasius. When refuting heretics, he does not petition the bishop of Rome, nor does he resort to appealing to tradition. Instead, Athanasius counters the Arians and their misinterpretation of Scripture through a proper and sound exegesis of the text and demonstrates the error of their conclusions. Today, Jehovah's Witnesses appeal to the same passages as did the Arians. Likewise, we respond in the same manner as Athanasius did in the fourth century when they show up at our door—by going directly to the Word and pointing out where they are wrong, and where they have made unwarranted conclusions.

But Athanasius did not merely stop with charging subordinationism is alien to the Scriptures. Taking his position a step further, the Alexandrian bishop wrote elsewhere, "For indeed the holy and God-breathed Scriptures are self-sufficient for the preaching of the truth."[4] Here, I submit, is the evangelical example apotheosized in its fullest. Athanasius could have utilized any source or appealed to any authority, yet the one supreme object to which he resorted was the "God-breathed Scriptures," testifying to its perspicuity. For Athanasius, the Bible was sufficient, so much so that he fully believed he could take on the greatest heresy of his day and prove victorious in the end. He could do this because of the clarity of its teachings.

3. Godfrey et. al., *Sola Scriptura: The Protestant Position on the Bible*, 47.
4. Ibid., 49.

The next time anyone argues that Scripture is insufficient or incapable of being properly understood apart from an infallible magisterium, it must be noted that the Holy Spirit's enlightening and the clearness of God's Word is enough to confront any aberrant point of view—just as Athanasius taught. After all, "the word of God is living and active, sharper than any two-edged sword, piercing to the division of soul and of spirit, of joints and of marrow, and discerning the thoughts and intentions of the heart" (Heb 4:12). God's people hear his voice. Just as Matthew's Gospel declares, the elect cannot be deceived (24:24).

It should be added that if the Arians were correct in their supposition that Christ was the highest and greatest of all God's creation, it would inevitably lead to untenable conclusions. For instance, God would not be directly involved in the salvation of his people. Put another way, salvation would cost God nothing. That is, he would have delegated, so to speak, the poignant and ignominious task of coming to earth and dying to save sinners. Would that be a truly loving act? It hardly seems so.

Another troubling issue the Arian controversy poses is whether or not a mere created being, however preeminent, could bring about salvation. When the totality of the biblical evidence is considered, there doesn't seem to be any way possible. A mere creature could not in any meaningful way begin to be able to satisfy the wrath of an infinite God and win back his favor. Only God can bring reconciliation with himself. That is why the Word became flesh and dwelt among mankind—in order to save his people from their sins (Matt 1:21).

There is a story of a judge who ruled fairly and always rendered justice in accordance with the law. Then, one day, a young man was brought before the court, because he had committed a serious offense. When the judge looked upon the defendant he was deeply saddened. He recognized his own son stood guilty before the judgment seat, but what was he to do? His mercy wanted to let his boy go unpunished, but justice demanded a penalty be paid. The judge did what only he could do in order to satisfy the debt owed—he declared the son guilty and ordered him to receive thirty lashes. As soon as he passed judgment, the judge stepped down from his position and instructed the guard to strike him instead. The judge received the punishment in his son's stead. The father paid the penalty he had demanded. Likewise, God is the only one who could satisfy his own sentence. Anyone less than God would be insufficient to meet the demand necessary to satisfy the judgment. Only God could make payment.

More than this, the deity of Christ is the only hope mankind has. If Jesus is not God, we are all to be pitied for deifying a mere mortal and placing Jesus on par with God. If Christ is not deity, then everyone who has bowed a knee and offered a prayer to him has been guilty of idolatry. Yet, Jesus gave no indication that he thought it unwarranted when people worshipped him. Furthermore, Jesus repeatedly forgave sins, an act God alone is able to do. The Jews of Jesus' own day recognized the audacity of these personal claims of deity and sought to kill him for blasphemy. If unbelievers recognized what Jesus claimed, why should any professing believer not accept as true his claims of deity?

When we search the Scriptures, it becomes strikingly clear that salvation is by grace alone through faith alone on account of Christ alone, because he is God. He is our hope and our Rock, the One to whom we can turn. Christ saves, and Christ alone. The Nicene Creed succinctly summed up the biblical teaching of the Trinity when it affirmed, "Jesus Christ, the only begotten of the Father before all worlds. God of God, Light of light, very God of very God, begotten, not made, being of one substance with the Father . . . We believe in the Holy Spirit . . ."

Indeed, as Athanasius contended, the Scriptures are clear concerning the nature of Christ, because the Word of God is comprehensible. Christ Jesus is God—the second Person of the Trinity, equal with God (and the Holy Spirit), and Savior of the world. It is to the Bible alone that we turn in reconciling disputes and overcoming heretical movements. Scripture is the final authority in all matters of faith and practice and is sufficient to equip believers for every good work, including recognizing the nature of the Son. Christ is God. That much we know from Scripture alone, and that is what Nicea stood for in the early fourth century.

As believers, then, we stand here today, believing the biblical truth about the Trinity, because the Christian faithful from centuries ago held firm in the face of opposition and would not deny the truth of who Christ is—the second person in the Trinity, coequal and coeternal with the Father and the Holy Spirit. We stand upon the shoulders of giants who have gone before us, preserving the faith as we received it and passing it along to the next generation of believers.

Think About It

1. Does the Bible clearly teach the deity of Christ?
2. Could you explain and defend the Incarnation of the Son to a non-Christian?
3. Why is it important to affirm that Jesus is God?
4. What verses do you know support the belief Jesus is God?
5. What theological ramifications are there if Jesus is not God?

4

Augustine of Hippo and the Pelagian Controversy

(354–430)

You might have heard the story of a group of theologians who were discussing the doctrines of predestination and free will. After the dialogue became heated, the dissenters broke off into two groups. One person, unable to make up his mind which party to join, made his way to the predestination supporters. When challenged why he was in their midst, he responded, "I came here of my own free will."

"Free will?!" the crowd shouted disbelievingly. "You don't belong in this group!"

So the man retreated to the opposing side and when asked why he switched, he responded, "I was sent here."

"Get out," they fumed. "Unless you came to us by your own free will, you cannot join us." The confused man didn't know what to do. Unsure where to go next or what to do, he was left out in the cold.

In an age of religion without much reflection, speculation about predestination and free will seems pointless. Feeling neither certain nor dogmatic about either position, most professing believers have simply not thought through the ramifications of embracing predestination or free will. The average twenty-first-century Christian, feeling uncertain about either side, would probably join with the man left out in the cold. Yet, the greatest theological minds in the history of the church wrestled with these doctrines and determined indifference is not a viable option; they touched the very heart of the gospel itself.

THE STRUGGLE FOR SPIRITUAL FREEDOM

"Pick up and read, pick up and read." These words, chanted by a young child from a nearby house, floated into the garden and pierced the troubled soul of a sobbing professor of rhetoric. Sitting under a fig tree, rivers streamed from the man's eyes as he repeatedly questioned, "How long, O Lord? How long, Lord, will you be angry to the uttermost? Do not be mindful of our old iniquities."[1]

The troubling "iniquities" to which this mournful individual specifically referred, and subsequently confessed, was his bondage to concupiscence. For the greater part of his life, Augustine—for that was the individual lamenting his sins—was unable to master his sexual drive. In fact, so intense were his desires to satisfy the flesh that he continued to find himself controlled by his illicit passions. Indeed, so strong was his desire to continue in licentious living that he prayed more than once, "Make me chaste, but not yet." So for Augustine, hearing the exhortation to read was a welcome relief.

Treating the incident as a divine command directly from heaven, the professor's demeanor suddenly changed, and he began thinking intently of what the command could mean. The only possible thought he could muster was that he should continue reading from the book he had in his possession. Now, he opened where he left off; his eyes fell upon the words which enlightened his soul:

> "Let us walk properly as in the daytime, not in orgies and drunkenness, not in sexual immorality and sensuality, not in quarreling and jealousy. But put on the Lord Jesus Christ, and make no provision for the flesh, to gratify its desires" (Rom 13:13–14).

He neither wished to read further nor needed to he later recalled in his spiritual autobiography. Responding to the Romans passage about personal responsibility and victory over sin, Augustine resolved to dedicate his life to serving the Lord. While he first attempted to find peace and light in Manicheanism and later through Neoplatonism, it was not until he placed his confidence in Christ Jesus that relief from all anxiety flooded his heart. Or, as he put it, "All the shadows of doubt were dispelled."[2] What he had been putting off for a long time was devoting himself to serving God. Now, however, things changed. He resolved to

---

1. Augustine, *Confessions*, 152.
2. Ibid., 153.

immerse himself in his newfound convictions, and his decision set him on a course that would eventually make him one of the most influential figures in the history of the church.

In order to better understand Augustine's struggle for freedom and the profound conversion in the garden at Milan, one must first trace the professor's footsteps to that point in time. Also important is to understand his background, which would prove instrumental in the expansion and articulation of doctrine that would eventually inspire future generations—ultimately culminating in the rediscovery of certain biblical doctrines in the early sixteenth century.

A TORTUOUS ODYSSEY TO FAITH

Augustine was born in 354 in the small town of Tagaste in North Africa (present day eastern Algeria) to a pagan father and a Christian mother. His father, a minor Roman official who also farmed a few acres, followed after the traditional pagan religion of the empire. By contrast, Augustine's mother, Monica, was a devout Christian who prayed fervently for the salvation of both her husband and son—an effort that was eventually rewarded. Augustine's relationship with his mother was deep and significant as she continued to play an important role in his life well after his adolescent years. His father, by contrast, is scarcely mentioned in Augustine's writings and does not seem to have had close ties with his son.

What both were aware of, nevertheless, was the exceptional intellectual aptitude Augustine displayed at an early age. Because he showed signs of great promise, his parents were committed to giving him the best education possible. To achieve this goal, they sent him to a nearby town and later to the larger city of Carthage where he would receive training in the greatest Latin-speaking region of Africa.

By the time he reached the metropolis at seventeen years of age, Augustine, though not totally devoid of intellectual pursuits, engaged in other, more sensual, interests the city offered. There he found an appetite for the flesh and took for himself a concubine who bore him a son. He named the boy Adeodatus. In total, Augustine lived with the girl for thirteen years, only dismissing her after he overcame his defiling passion. His insatiable appetite for indulging the flesh lucidly demonstrated his inability to escape his sin, which he only later realized after God rescued him by grace.

When Augustine was not engaged in worldly activities and instead committed himself to his studies, he succeeded brilliantly. At first he was content to study the discipline of rhetoric, hoping to become like one of the great orators. Eventually, he came into contact with a treatise by Cicero, the Latin author, who argued that one must also seek after truth. So impressed with his writings was he that Augustine reached the conclusion that mellifluous speech was not enough. One needed to know truth as well. Accordingly, the pursuit of ultimate truth became Augustine's new mission. His search first led him to the Bible and to the teachings of his youth, but to him, learned in style and erudition, Scripture seemed crude and barbaric—especially the Old Testament.

The quest for truth next led the young student to Manicheism, a religion whose origins were traced to a man named Mani who taught in Persia but died a martyr's death of crucifixion around the year 276. Similar to Gnosticism, Mani advocated the fundamental belief that within the universe resides an ongoing conflict of two powers: the one, good and the other, evil. Humankind is a mixture of both, the soul being good and the physical body, evil. The measure of every individual, therefore, was to free the good entrapped inside the evil, a task that could only be successfully achieved through prayer, meditation, and abstinence from such enjoyments as wine, meats, wealth, lusts, procreation, and other similar pursuits. According to Mani, the idea of salvation was revealed to a long list of prophets and sages, including Buddha, Zoroaster, Jesus and, of course, to Mani as well.

Augustine remained committed to the teachings of Mani for nine years, partly due to the inherently mocking tone it exhibited toward the Christian Bible for its so-called inelegant writings. Augustine was also attracted to Manicheism because he believed it offered the best answer to some of his perplexing concerns, namely, the origin of evil. Augustine was taught by his mother there was only one God, yet evil resided all around him. So how could the God of Christianity be the supreme God of the universe? If God is the creator of all things, as Monica taught him, how could he be good as the church insisted? Augustine was not yet convinced. Instead, Manicheism, as best he could tell, offered the only satisfactory answers.

But things would eventually change. Seeds of dissatisfaction with Mani's teachings germinated in his mind. When Augustine started to vent his doubts openly at a public gathering, he was promised that a great teacher, Faustus, could assuage all doubts and answer all his questions. When the time finally arrived for Augustine to meet the sage, he, like so many others, turned out to be a grave disappointment. Doubts concerning the veracity of Mani's philosophical speculations only increased. About the time of the pinnacle of his struggle with Manicheanism, Augustine's friends convinced him to move to Rome where a career seemed more promising. A year later, in 384, he found himself in Milan where he secured a teaching position at the university.

Living in Milan encouraged Augustine's journey from Manicheanism to the philosophy of the third century thinker, Plotinus. Neoplatonism—as it was called—was a popular philosophical belief at the time with religious overtones. Similar to Manicheism in some respects, Neoplatonism differed from the former in that it affirmed the One, the source of all being. Unlike Mani's teachings, Neoplatonism distinguished itself by affirming only one good principle, and from that principle, all reality is derived through emanations, similar to watching concentric circles appear on the surface of a pond after an object is dropped. The closer one is to the center, the purer one is; conversely, the farther away from the circle one is the more inferior he becomes. Evil, therefore, originates, not from the source of the One, but from moving further away from the One. This seemed to better answer Augustine's question concerning the origins of evil. Stated another way, evil is not "something," but rather, moving away from the goodness of the ultimate.

Despite embracing the more sophisticated Neoplatonism, Augustine still harbored some doubt about the veracity of its claims. Then there was the other issue of his mother—who resided with him in Milan—who insisted he attend the sermons of the city bishop, a man named Ambrose. As a professor of rhetoric, Augustine was curious to study the famous speaker's style. What eventually amazed him was that Christianity could be both intellectual and eloquent. More than this, he also came to realize the "troubling passages" of the Old Testament could be interpreted allegorically. His attendance at first was purposeful in that he went to hear Ambrose solely to study his elocution, yet, as time passed, he listened more as a seeker of truth than as an academician. Christianity finally seemed palatable.

Then came the final impetus when a friend told him the story of Anthony, the famous Egyptian ascetic monk, who was capable of withstanding all sorts of temptations. This made Augustine ashamed at his own lack of self-control. If unlearned hermits could be victorious in the face of myriad trials, how could he, with his superior academic training, not be able to achieve similar results as well? His sense of sin troubled him so greatly that he found himself one day reading, alone, in a garden.

It was at this moment that his troubles culminated in the tearful lament alluded to earlier. He was grossly ashamed of his concupiscence and conscious of his sins. Tears streaming down his face, he dropped his Bible, only to hear the melodious voice of a child singing, "Pick up and read, pick up and read."

The following Easter, in 387, Augustine, accompanied by his friend, Alypius, and son, Adeodatus, was baptized by Ambrose in Milan. Now a changed man, Augustine resigned from his teaching post and resolved to return to North Africa to spend the remainder of his life. He took with him his mother and son, leaving behind his concubine of thirteen years. On the return journey, Monica took ill and died. Overcome with grief, Augustine stayed in Rome for several months. By the autumn of 388, he arrived with his son in Tagaste, only to lose him to illness, adding to his already fragile state of mind. He sought to isolate himself from the world, but God had other plans for him. His keen mind and natural leadership abilities were quickly recognized in the church, and the bishop was eager to enlist his services.

After three years, Augustine—albeit against his will—was ordained a priest in the church at Hippo. Soon thereafter, the bishop, Valerius, convinced him to serve as an assistant bishop in the city. For four years, Augustine faithfully served Valerius until the bishop died, leaving Augustine, the former Manichean and Neoplatonist, at the helm of the church. For the next thirty-three years, Augustine would stand against great threats and controversies within the church to become one of the most influential ecclesiastical figures—one that shaped both Roman Catholic theology and Protestant thought.

THEOLOGIAN OF THE WESTERN CHURCH

One of the major controversies with which Augustine was forced to deal was the lingering issue of Donatism. By the time Augustine ascended into the office of bishop, the controversy was nearly a century old. Nevertheless, the issue remained at the forefront of many minds and was an issue that could not be avoided. The reader will recall the horrific persecution of Diocletian. It was during his reign of terror that some bishops handed over the Scriptures to Roman authorities for fear of punishment or death. In so doing, Donatus and his followers argued, the bishops were guilty of apostasy and did not deserve to be included in Christ's church. Moreover, the Donatists believed they comprised the true church and not the catholic church in which the bishops operated.

The Donatists further concluded that all bishops who handed over Scripture or recanted were "unworthy," and as such, the sacraments they conferred to the people were ineffectual. That is, Donatists argued the validity of the sacraments depend upon the moral character of the presiding minister. To this vexing dilemma, then, Augustine responded that the legitimacy of a rite does not depend upon the one administering the sacrament but upon the person receiving it. Otherwise, people would live in perpetual fear that their baptism was invalid and would remain suspicious of the Lord's Supper. So on this point, the Western church agreed with Augustine, who was instrumental in developing a sacerdotal view of the church (God's grace is channeled through the administration of sacraments via priests). That unfortunate view ultimately gave rise to many extremes of the Roman Catholic Church, especially during the medieval ages.

Another profound issue that resonated with the church in the West was Augustine's development of the concept of "just war". It was his staunch defense of the universal church in the Donatist controversy that led him to some regrettable conclusions regarding theological foes. Initially opposed to the idea of using force to coerce his rivals, Augustine sought refuge and justification for physical persuasion in Jesus' parable in which he said, "Compel people to come in, that my house may be filled" (Luke 14:23). By the unfortunate misinterpretation of a single theologian,[3] later (professing) believers used his "just war" principle and waged conflict against Christian dissenters, most notably, during the age of the Inquisition.

While the aforementioned incidents in Augustine's life speak more to his belief in the importance of an organized church structure, the Pelagian controversy is, without question, the most important theologi-

3. Due to Augustine's preeminent standing in the churches of North Africa, his belief that the Donatists could be physically compelled since the purpose was driven by a properly instituted authority out of love for truth and not for political or territorial gain was adopted and embraced by later generations.

cal aspect concerning the development and refinement of the Christian emphasis on sin and grace. It was against Pelagius that Augustine penned his most significant theological treatise on the nature of man and the goodness of God—a work that would prove instrumental in the theology of later men such as Luther, Zwingli, and Calvin.

The beginnings of the Pelagian controversy transpired when Pelagius, a British monk, took umbrage with Augustine's famous prayer: "Grant what Thou commandest, and command what Thou dost desire." Augustine's point was simply that if God expected something from him, God would first have to grant what was expected. In and of himself, Augustine was constrained by his own sinfulness to keep even the most basic commands of God. Pelagius, by contrast, was appalled by the concept of grace being a divine gift and necessary in order to perform what God commands. Such an idea implies that mankind does not have the ability to obey God unless he gives people this gift. For the pious monk, responsibility must necessarily entail ability. Otherwise, God would not command people to do something for which they do not have the capacity. Stated another way, Pelagius taught that if God requires mankind to obey his laws then it naturally follows that mankind necessarily possesses the moral ability to obey apart from divine intercession. And, in light of the other doctrines he rejected, it is not far-fetched to see how the monk could reach this conclusion.

Pelagius denied the concept of original sin, that is, that all humanity inherited Adam's sin. Instead, he argued that humans are able to act freely and righteously if they choose to do so. Pelagius believed and taught that the Christian life was an ongoing process and a constant effort in which one could overcome evil in the world and attain salvation. There is no inherited, corrupt nature, he argued, and no one sins until individuals, of their own free will, decide to do so. Pelagius did, however, agree with Augustine in that God made creatures free and that evil originated with the will. So for Pelagius, sin was something that could be overcome through personal effort. Without this ability to sin or not to sin, personal transgressions could be readily excused.

This teaching stood at open variance with Augustine's own experience. He recalled his own personal plight in which he constantly waged war with the flesh but was unable to conquer his desires even though, at times, he desperately wanted to do so. Thus, Pelagius was oversimplifying the issue of the human will, because as life had taught Augustine, the will does not always have the will to do what is right. According to the bishop of Hippo, man has free will but lacks liberty. The power of sin is so great that it has taken the will captive for all humankind since the fall of Adam. Sinners can will to act, but those actions, apart from grace, will only result in sinful choices. In other words, humanity can freely will and choose, but is never capable of choosing to do what is morally right.

This, however, does not mean freedom is lost. As Augustine stressed over and over again, the sinner is still free to choose among various alternatives but is only able to choose sin. That is to say, fallen man has not lost his ability to make choices. Rather, it just means that when given the opportunity to make those choices he will choose selfishly, deciding according to the desire of his spoiled heart. Prior to the fall in the Garden of Eden, Adam and Eve were free to sin though they lived in a perfect state. But after both chose to disobey God, the freedom that once resided in humanity was and is no longer available because of the consequences of their actions. Instead, humans, in their natural condition, and apart from the grace of God, are only able to choose according to their post-fall nature. As Augustine noted, the only true freedom remaining in natural man is the freedom to sin. When God redeems the lost, the will is freed from its state of bondage and only then is capable of doing what is morally pleasing to the Lord. Eventually, in a future glorified state in heaven, believers will continue to be free, but this time they will only be free *not* to sin.

Returning to the moment of conversion, Augustine made it clear that even the decision to accept grace is not left with the individual. Since sinners are slaves to sin, they would never, under any given circumstance, even begin to accept grace when granted the opportunity if they are still "at enmity toward God." Therefore, the initiative in conversion is not of human origin but divine in totality. Grace is irresistible because of its origin, and it is always efficacious to those who have been preordained to be recipients of this special, undeserved favor.

So how did the church respond to the Augustinian-Pelagian controversy? After several years of ongoing debate and copious writings on both sides of the issue, Pelagianism was rejected because of its radical views. Denying the effects of the fall and the nature of sin—effects which are displayed so obviously in infants—was too great of a practical issue to dismiss so easily. But that is not to say that Christians wholly embraced

Augustine's teaching on the nature of man and salvation. Augustine's views were not heralded as universally orthodox. Opposition came against Augustine for his denying human participation in the salvific process. Some even called his soteriology (doctrine of salvation) innovative and new. What resulted from attacking his position was a sort of compromise between the two sides, sometimes called semi-Pelagianism. These individuals accepted Augustine's position of original sin and the corruption of the will but refused to carry the position to its logical conclusion and go as far as Augustine.

Ironically, after nearly a century of wrestling with these issues, many theologians adopted the term "Augustinian" while redefining what it meant by rejecting his views on the predestination of sinners and irresistible grace. In 529, the Synod of Orange officially rejected Pelagianism and gave its approbation to Augustinianism, albeit an adulterated version of his teachings. It would not be until many centuries later, with some exceptions, that theologians interpreted Augustine as he actually taught and crystallized his teachings in a systematic fashion. Their articulation of Augustinian thought served as the basis for justification and proved to be at the foundation of teachings that threatened the entire structure of Roman Catholic doctrine.

Getting back to Augustine, the publication of his monumental *City of God* remains one of Augustine's most influential works—and the one he considered his masterpiece. Written over a span of fourteen years and contained in twenty-two books, the impetus for his work was the sack of Rome by Goths in the year 410. The once seemingly indomitable empire, the impregnable city of Rome that ruled most of the civilized world for centuries, was in rapid decline. Astonishment flooded the minds of its inhabitants, soon followed by rumors and accusations that the Christians were responsible for the empire's destruction.

Disturbed by the growing sentiment, a Roman official in North Africa wrote to Augustine, relating the charges against Christianity and asking him to write a refutation. Augustine obliged and penned a massive, encyclopedic history of the empire in which he argued there are essentially two cities—one built with a foundation of love for self and the other built with a foundation of love for God. The two constitute two radically divergent worldviews and are irreconcilable. In the end, only the latter will survive. Human history is replete with kings and kingdoms built upon a movable foundation and, like everything in life, wither away. Only the city of God will withstand the test of time. The destruction of the Roman Empire, he argued, was just punishment for the rampant wickedness inherent throughout the land.

Augustine survived four years after the completion of his *City of God*. He was never able to escape the coming invasion of foreign hordes even in his own home land. When Augustine died in 430, Vandals were at the gates of Hippo, bringing change to a land once ruled by the great and mighty Roman Empire.

Though Germanic invaders brought destruction to the city, his life's works were providentially spared during the siege. In addition to his voluminous writings on sin, grace, and salvation, other biblical writings on the Trinity and commentaries on Scripture are unequaled in the early church and were the most prized writings of many of the humanistic scholars of the Renaissance. Indeed, no other early Christian of the first few centuries was more quoted than he. Augustine was eventually given the honorable title of "Doctor of the Church," and he was, by far, the favorite theologian of the Protestant Reformation. Both Roman Catholics and Protestants laud his work in the early church, and each readily attests to the reality that no other theologian since the apostle Paul, up to that point, influenced the Western church in a similar way.

AUGUSTINE AND THE DOCTRINES OF GRACE

More than a millennia before the term Calvinism was introduced to the church, Augustine contended for the veracity of God's sovereignty in the salvation of sinners. For so doing, one of his opponents, namely, Vincent of Lerins, argued Augustine's conclusion should be rejected, because his doctrine of salvation was not believed "everywhere, always, and by all."[4]

For Augustine, however, the question was not a matter of whether the majority of professing Christians accepted his understanding of God's role in salvation, but rather, what the Bible taught. The entire world could go astray and follow after a lie, but the Word of God was a firm foundation that never vacillated or changed with the seasons. The

---

4. Ironically, many Roman Catholics to this day appeal to Lerins' response when answering certain evangelical doctrines. Yet, when confronted with the reality that many dogmas required on the *de fide* basis are without historical merit, some are not above resorting to John Henry Cardinal Newman's "development hypothesis" when discussing such non-biblical concepts as the Immaculate Conception, the Assumption of Mary, papal infallibility, and so on. If the same argument can be used against the Roman Catholic Church's positions, then it is not a valid argument. Inconsistency is a sign of a failed argument.

unchanging reality of Scripture serves as the final rule of faith to function in Christ's church. And that, of course, is why Augustine appealed to the text before reaching a conclusion over against counting the number of adherents of any given position. Even with that said, the question remains: Does the Bible actually confirm what Augustine believed and taught? Does God save a particular people perfectly, or does mankind allow God to save? Does Scripture speak of natural humans in bondage to sin without the capacity for performing good deeds? Are humans, to use a colloquial term, truly "totally depraved"?

One perennial issue true in Augustine's day—that remains true today as well—is that many incorrectly assume the use of "radical depravity" or "total depravity" implies that all humans everywhere are as bad as they could be. Objectors point to the charitable works of Muslims, Buddhists, and Atheists—to name just a few—as proof that people perform good works apart from the belief in the God of Christianity. But this, of course, is simply a false attack against what is actually meant by the term. The Westminster Confession of Faith defines the doctrine succinctly,

> "Man, by his fall into a state of sin, hath wholly lost all ability of will to any spiritual good accompanying salvation; so as a natural man, being altogether averse from good, and dead in sin, is not able, by his own strength, to convert himself, or to prepare himself thereunto."

Put another way, man's depravity is total in that there is no aspect of man, be it body, mind, or will, that was unaffected by the fall. It is total in the case of our rebellion against God and in our rebellion against righteousness.

There is a popular myth circulating in evangelical churches today that goes something like this: Mankind is earnestly searching after God. The reality, though, is something far different. As Augustine eventually discovered when working through Romans and confirmed in his own struggle for purity:

> "There is none righteous, not even one; there is none who understands, there is none who seeks for God; all have turned aside, together they have become useless; there is none who does good, there is not even one" (Rom 3:10–12).

Paul indicates there are no God-seekers. This passage alone should prove sufficient in demonstrating there is no delight in the holiness of God apart from his grace.

This is not to say, however, that totally sinful men cannot be religious. In fact, they can be very much so—some even more than professing Christians. Presumably, we all know of people who live upright lives but deny the Maker. The difference, though, is that such individuals are not seeking after the one true God. The reality is that they have suppressed the sensus divinitus and are searching to please the god of their imaginations, because they are under the power of sin (Rom 3:9). People might "seek" God as a way to protect them from death or suffering or to enhance their temporal blessings. But these good acts are performed for selfish reasons. We are told "whatever is not from faith is sin" (Rom 14:23). Many are eager to credit unbelievers with good works, but God is the one who judges. He has already declared "all of us have become like one who is unclean, and all our righteous deeds are like a filthy garment" (Isa 64:6). Just because someone appears to be seeking does not mean he has the innate ability or desire, apart from grace, to do so.

The apostle Paul gives as his starting point the fact that all of mankind has sinned in Adam (Rom 5:12). This is what theologians call federal representation. That is, the Lord views this first man, Adam, as the representative of the entire human race. Unfortunately for humanity, Adam plunged his posterity into a condition where they are now "dead in trespasses and sin" (Eph 2:1). All humans are consequently without excuse before God (Rom 2:1), because all have sinned and have fallen short of the glory of God (Rom 3:23). Paul elsewhere confirms this idea when he wrote to the Ephesians "remember that you were at that time separate from Christ, excluded from the commonwealth of Israel, and strangers to the covenants of promise, having no hope and without God in the world" (Eph 2:12). Sinners are without hope apart from the goodness and mercy of God.

Since the fall, humans are by nature children of wrath (Eph 2:3) and are utterly indisposed and disabled in regard to all that which is good. Paul says only evil inclinations originate from them. The apostle also tells us "the mind set on the flesh is hostile toward God; for it does not subject itself to the law of God, for it is not even able to do so" (Rom 8:7). Compare these words with those of Jesus who taught, "This is the judgment, that the Light has come into the world, and men loved the darkness rather than the Light, for their deeds were evil" (John 3:19).

Even a cursory study of biblical anthropology reveals that humanity has a bias against God and will always choose freely and willingly that which is evil. Think for a moment what this means. With respect to matters of righteousness, mankind will not, because he cannot, do what God commands. John tells us that the one who commits sin is the slave of sin (John 8:34). The picture the apostle is painting is that those who sin are taken captive by their master, sin, and are unable to deliver themselves from bondage. It is as if one is a prisoner with an iron band chained around his leg. He cannot break free from that weighty shackle (nor does he desire to do so). On the contrary; every sin committed tightens that band. The more one sins, the greater the enslavement becomes. Yet, as sobering as this statement is it is lucidly attested elsewhere.

Consider, "those who are in the flesh cannot please God" (Rom 8:8). The person who is still "in the flesh"—the unbeliever—is *unable* to submit himself to the law of God. The idea that humans can believe in Christ or be enlightened to the gospel message apart from divine illumination is contrary to the whole of Scripture. Believing is a good act that pleases God, but as the Bible clearly and overwhelmingly indicates, unbelievers "cannot please God". The sinner is constantly at hostility toward the Creator, and so long as there are unresolved sin issues, how can an unbeliever "choose" to do what is right? Paul makes the answer abundantly clear—the unregenerate sinner cannot. The unregenerate man lacks the will or ability to please God, to repent, to believe in Christ, to turn from his sins, or to embrace the cross. He must first be raised spiritually in order to do these things that are pleasing to God.

Listen to the words of Jesus, "No one can come to Me unless the Father who sent Me draws him; and I will raise him up on the last day" (John 6:44). This passage is a clear indictment against the notion of autonomous human volition to freely choose righteousness—*No one can come to Me*.

Now some have tried to explain this passage away by interpreting the verse to mean that Jesus "woos" sinners to himself. Such an interpretation, however, does violence to the text. The Greek verb translated here as "draw" is used also in the book of Acts. "But when her masters saw that their hope of profit was gone, they seized Paul and Silas and *dragged* them into the market place before the authorities" (Acts 16:19). Paul and Silas were not *wooed* into the market, but they were *dragged*. That is, they were compelled to appear before the authorities. John uses the same Greek term when he describes God's action in calling sinners. God does not woo sinners but draws them irresistibly to himself. It is hard to imagine anything more amazing. This is nothing short of a true testimony of God's love because the "natural man does not accept the things of the Spirit of God, for they are foolishness to him; and he cannot understand them, because they are spiritually appraised" (1 Cor 2:14). God must give sinners the desire to come, otherwise they would never do so apart from the efficacious power of the Holy Spirit.

Just as the Ethiopian cannot change his skin, nor can the leopard his spots (Jer 13:23), the sinner cannot change his ways through his own efforts. Genuine and everlasting change transcends the ability of mankind. Our only hope is a change brought by the sovereign power and regenerating work of the Holy Spirit. The next time we have an inclination to think more highly of ourselves than we ought, we would do well to remember the biblical concept of humanity. That is to say, we do not possess the power of self-regeneration, and until an inward change happens, we remain enemies with God. Remember that it was God who promised, "I will give you a new heart and put a new spirit within you; and I will remove the heart of stone from your flesh and give you a heart of flesh" (Ezek 36:26). So the reason sinners are changed at all and some come to love the Lord is because of God's promise to deliver his people from their sins (Matt 1:21)—and not because one exercised his own ability to choose God.

In summary, Augustine's understanding of "total depravity" refers to mankind's absolute rebellion towards his Maker in that everything he does is in opposition to God. Remaining in this desperate condition will ultimately lead to only one destiny—being eternally separated from him. If unbelievers do not first see themselves for what they truly are, how, then, can they turn away from their sins and embrace Christ—let alone grasp the goodness, grace, and mercy of God in the redemptive plan of salvation? Once sinners humble themselves to this biblical truth of total depravity, they will then better understand what it means to declare that salvation is of the Lord (Jonah 2:9).

So to conclude, the biblical concept of free will is that man retains the freedom to choose what he desires—but that his desires are wicked and self-serving and, if left in an unregenerate state, he will never choose Christ. The sinner cannot choose Christ, because there is no desire in his heart for God. The fall left mankind in this desperate state, and it is only through the effectual grace of the Lord, working in the hearts of men, that the unregenerate can come to a saving faith. Once God works his grace in the hearts of his chosen people, their desires are fundamentally changed. Then, and only then, are people able to receive God as their personal savior. When one accepts Jesus as Lord and Savior, he only does so because the Lord first took away his heart of stone and replaced it with a heart of flesh (Ezek 36:26).

Augustine understood the importance of this doctrine and recognized the inherent problems with rejecting this fundamental teaching. Remove God from the salvific process and the glory that is rightly due him is robbed, regardless of all objections to the contrary. For this very reason, Augustine wrote voluminously in response to Pelagius. It was his guiding influence that shaped the foundation of the Protestant Reformation.

Before Luther and Calvin, there was Augustine—fighting for God's absolute sovereignty over his creation and articulating the reality of God's predestinating love. B. B. Warfield said it best when he remarked, "It is Augustine who gave us the Reformation." Indeed, Augustine enunciated the truths first expressed by Christ and later, Paul. Though the bishop of Hippo gave impetus to the doctrines of grace, it would take another millennium before an Augustinian monk living in the sixteenth century set the world ablaze through the proclamation of God's sovereignty in the salvation of sinners—a doctrine that remains vital for believers today.

Think About It

1. Why are discussions concerning predestination and free will relevant?
2. Do you think that human pride has any part in the rejection of total depravity?
3. What do Jesus and Paul each say about the nature of the human will since the fall?
4. How is the unbeliever's volition changed?
5. Since God is sovereign over all aspects of life, both good and bad, how do you react when you face difficult times or severe testing? Do you complain about your elected leaders, the economy, your job, your coworkers, and so on? Before you give an answer, read Romans 8:28.

5

The Crusades

(1095–1291)

In May of 2009, Eastern Nazarene College, located on Boston's historic south shore, officially announced the name of their new mascot, dropping "Crusaders," because of increasing negative connotations that have, in recent years, become emblematic of religious intolerance and fanatical zeal against Muslims. Like other institutions of higher learning in America, the college mascot was changed in order to express the reality that Christianity is a community, not of medieval, religious fanaticism, but of love. The outcry from faculty, students, and alumni was so strong in opposition to the Crusader mascot, the college opted to use a lion—much as C. S. Lewis did in his classic works—to better represent Christian ideals and the religious connotations of strength and courage.

The prevalent attitude at Eastern Nazarene College is not anomalous. Indeed, growing pessimism toward the religious wars of the twelfth and thirteenth centuries were captured lucidly in the BBC series *The Crusaders*. Though not without its own political agenda, the series portrays the crusades as a long-term movement of the medieval period in which Christians waged a misguided war of intolerance against the sophisticated and peaceful Islamic world. As it is, such oversimplifications and anachronistic readings of history are gaining popular support among the denizens of both Europe and North America, but the truth of the matter is far more complex.

Without falling into the same trap that has ensnared so many others while explaining origins of the conflicts, the crusades must be understood in the context of a host of factors including European feudalism, expanding papal power, ecclesiastical reform, gallant and knightly chivalry, and the tumultuous relationship between the Eastern and Western branches of the church, among a myriad of other influences. The crusades were also, if not predominantly, in reaction to expanding Islamic domination and conquests that began in the early decades of the seventh century. By the close of the eleventh century, Muslim expansion covered nearly three-quarters of what used to be "Christian lands". Islamic expansion that began during Muhammad's day continued until it culminated in expeditions that occupied the attention of millions of Europeans for more than two centuries.

In all, there were seven numbered crusades, the first beginning in 1095 and the final one terminating in 1291 with the fall of Acre. Between these years were numerous other expeditions and journeys to the Promised Land, most of which ended in tragedy and bitter disappointment as amply demonstrated in one of the most poignant events of the era, the Children's Crusade.

A CALL TO ARMS—THE FIRST CRUSADE

At the Council of Clermont in southern France in 1095, fourteen archbishops, two-hundred and fifty bishops, four-hundred abbots, and thousands of spectators gathered to listen to Pope Urban II address the multitude in the open air. Urban, a Frenchman himself, implored his fellow countrymen to take up arms in support of the Christian religion "against the barbarians". Appealing to the doctrine of "just war" and the actions of those who preceded him—namely, Constantine, as well as Charlemagne and his son, Lewis, who expanded the church through military prowess—Urban spoke these words:

> "For, as the most of you have heard, the Turks and Arabs have attacked them and have conquered the territory of Romania [the Greek empire] as far west as the shore of the Mediterranean and the Hellespont, which is called the Arm of St. George. They have occupied more and more of the lands of those Christians, and have overcome them in seven battles. They have killed and captured many, and have destroyed the churches and devastated the empire. If you permit them to continue thus for awhile with impurity, the faithful of God will be much more widely attacked by them. On this account I, or rather the Lord, beseech you as Christ's heralds to publish this everywhere and to persuade all people of whatever rank, foot-soldiers and knights, poor and rich, to carry aid promptly to those Christians and to destroy

that vile race from the lands of our friends. I say this to those who are present, it is meant also for those who are absent. Moreover, Christ commands it.

All who die by the way, whether by land or by sea, or in battle against the pagans, shall have immediate remission of sins. This I grant them through the power of God with which I am invested. O what a disgrace if such a despised and base race, which worships demons, should conquer a people which has the faith of omnipotent God and is made glorious with the name of Christ! With what reproaches will the Lord overwhelm us if you do not aid those who, with us, profess the Christian religion!"[1]

Though the call to military action was nothing new, the time prior to the council was not yet ripe for such decisive action on a large scale. Yet, when Urban finished his impassioned plea for assistance, his hearers greeted him with chants of *"Deus vult, Deus vult"*—God wills it, God wills it. Attitudes had changed, and the prevailing sentiment of holy war—akin to the religious conquests of Joshua and Gideon in ancient days—was gaining rapid acceptance.

Combine this with the reality that by the end of the eleventh-century, Europe witnessed difficult times. Crops failed, diseases plagued humanity, and the majority living on the continent labored in the shackles of servitude to nobility. So the call to venture into foreign lands as soldiers of Christ, therefore, was received with great zeal by peasants and aristocracy alike. Based on the council, the primary goal of the crusades was simple: the conquest of the Holy Land and the defeat of Islamic invaders.

The reader would do well to remember that soon after the expansion of Christianity, Jerusalem became holy ground. Old Testament localities of prominence and the area of Jesus' ministry were considered sacrosanct. Pilgrims from across the globe ventured to catch a glimpse of the location of the crucifixion, the tomb in which the Lord was buried, and the area where Jesus ascended into heaven. Jerome, Augustine, and Gregory of Nyssa were just a few of the many Christian scholars who emphasized the nearness of God in Jerusalem.

---

1. See Thatcher and McNeal, *A Source Book for Medieval History*, 513–17. In addition to this report, four other accounts of Pope Urban II's speech at Clermont are recorded, including a report by Robert the Monk, Balderic of Dol, Guibert de Nogent, and the *Gesta* version.

Christian journeys to the Holy Land steadily increased. A visit to the land where Christ dwelt filled the imagination of millions. To be baptized in the same body of water in which Jesus was submerged or to set eyes on the places he tread was considered a sacred enterprise. Returning pilgrims increased awe and mystique with accounts of their journeys. Soon, special laws were enacted to facilitate travel. Hospitals and other places of rest were built along the route to provide comfort to weary travelers. In short, pilgrimages became profitable, both spiritually and monetarily.

Even though Jerusalem was conquered in 637 by Muslims, pilgrimages to the land were not severely disrupted until sultans from Egypt took control of the region almost four centuries later. In 1010, persecution against travelers broke out but abated soon thereafter. Even though physical violence was not necessarily a grave concern, pious tourists were, nevertheless, required to pay a toll in order to enter the city. Then, suddenly and without warning, the Seljuk Turks prohibited Christian pilgrimages to Jerusalem. A cruel and barbarous tribe by all accounts, they indiscriminately captured, imprisoned, or sold travelers into slavery. Those who escaped the Seljuk machinations returned to Europe with sordid tales of persecution and woe, flaming passions and righteous indignation.

The other, and lesser, cause for immediate action was an appeal from the Greek emperor. Islamic invasions continued to gain a stronghold in many Christian territories in the East. The bishop of Rome saw his opportunity to reunite the fractured Eastern branch of the church that had only recently endured the Great Schism in 1054.[2] Pressed by invaders, the hegemony of the region in the East was in question and a united front against invaders could help in resolving tensions in that area.

All of this combined to result in thousands flocking to join the ranks of crusaders who were ready and willing to take up the cross and fight the invaders. Urban's message, however, would only extend so far. After that, he needed messengers who could carry his appeal to other parts

---

2. Relations between the East and West had long been enmeshed prior to 1054, stemming from ecclesiastical and political differences between the Latin branch (West) of the church and the Greek (East). Officially, the dividing line was over the issue of *filioque*—a term used in the West that describes the relationship of the Spirit as proceeding from both the Father and the Son, whereas the East affirmed the Spirit proceeded from only the former. Other differences included elements of the Eucharist, papal jurisdiction, and the importance of Constantinople, among other issues.

of Europe. Chief among his followers was a man known as Peter the Hermit. History records that Peter was a dynamic speaker whose ability to persuade the masses was unmatched in his day. Riding throughout the countryside on a donkey, his face emaciated and his clothes in tatters, Peter's eloquence and ability to stir the passions of his fellow citizens made him one of the most successful evangelists and politicians at that time. Soon, people treated the hermit as divine, and some even went so far as to pluck the hairs from his donkey as keepsakes to be preserved as relics. Indeed, no other preacher of the crusading era could match his ability to spellbind an audience and convince them the Muslim atrocities committed against Christian travelers provided a legitimate impetus for stopping Islamic advances and retaking the Holy Land. It was as if, by the spring of 1096, all of Europe stood united in a common and holy purpose, headed by the bishop of Rome.

The date set by the council for departure was to be August 15, 1096, the Feast of the Assumption, but the excitement aroused by Peter the Hermit and others precluded the possibility of waiting so long. A disorganized throng, numbering greater than forty-thousand under the leadership of Peter, banded together and set out for Jerusalem. Along the way, however, they encountered robbery and massacre from other Europeans in search of loot, and by the time they reached the Emperor Alexius in Constantinople, their numbers had dwindled to seven-thousand. Once there, a false rumor circulated that the capital of the Islamic Turks in Nicea was captured by Christians. Eager to partake of the victory, the remaining few thousand were lured into a trap and, surrounded by an overwhelming force, were massacred by the Turkish cavalry.

Another rogue expedition consisting of some fifteen-thousand crusaders, under the leadership of German authority, met a similar and tragic end when they were ambushed and killed by the Hungarians.

In all, the pre-expeditions were very costly in number of fatalities. Nineteenth-century church historian, Philip Schaff, recorded that preliminary endeavors prior to the regular army resulted in the loss of some three-hundred thousand lives.[3]

The formal crusade, according to the lowest recorded numbers, included at least the same number of men who died in the preliminary excursions. Differing groups, some led by bishops and others by nobility, progressed through Europe until they united at Constantinople in

---

3. Schaff, 5:103.

Turkey. After fierce fighting, Nicea was captured, and the Turks were routed. Moving south toward Jerusalem, the crusaders were stalled in Antioch where success was elusive, with hardship and privations the norm. Soldiers were compelled to eat horses, dogs, camels, mice, and some, even worse. As difficult as the hunger was, thirst made the suffering even more acute. Malnutrition and starvation led to discouragement, and scores of crusaders began to doubt the wisdom of the pope's expedition.

Then their energies were revived when someone had a vision that the holy lance which pierced Christ's side was buried in Antioch. The chaplain who experienced the vision told them where to dig. As good fortune would have it, they made the miraculous discovery just as the chaplain had predicted. Convinced the unearthing of the lance was a sign from God, the men were reinvigorated to battle, fighting victoriously over against the much larger army.

Pressing onward after the victory at Antioch, the crusaders finally faced the Muslim-defended walls of Jerusalem. Intense fighting ensued. Boiling pitch and massive rocks were thrown at the besiegers in an attempt to keep them at bay. Contemplating a long siege, the Arabs poisoned the surrounding wells and razed the lands to deny the crusaders basic sustenance. Dead horses and decaying carcasses made life outside the walls almost unbearable. And with news of Muslim reinforcements only a few days away, the crusaders knew they needed to attack at once. Finally, almost as if by divine intervention, a fleet of supplies and tools found its way to the weary travelers.

Revived and refreshed, the crusaders chose Friday, the day of the crucifixion, for the final assault on the city. Resistance was fierce at first, but the soldiers, accompanied by a golden cross, were able to muster enough resolve to climb to the top of the city walls and gain a stronghold in the breach. Resistance slowly faded away, and the crusaders swept into the city, not as Christian victors, but as crusading knights with visions of absolute annihilation.

What ensued within the city walls was a bloodbath. Women were raped, pagans were slain. Synagogues were burned to the ground, with the greatest slaughter happening within the temple enclosure. It was even reported—with a touch of hyperbole, no doubt—that the massacre was so great people were wading up to their knees in the blood of the victims.

After their victory, the crusaders eased their consciences by travelling to the church of the Holy Sepulcher and offering up prayers and thanksgiving. With pious devotions completed, the massacre resumed. Not even the tears of women and children spared them a fatal destiny. As if that were not bad enough, the few prisoners captured were forced to remove all the dead bodies and blood from the streets for fear of pestilence.

William of Tyre (c. 1130–1186) said of the incident, "They cut down with sword every one whom they found in Jerusalem and spared no one. The victors were covered with blood from head to foot."[4] Then, only a few moments later he commented on the devotion of the crusaders. "It was a most affecting sight which filled the heart with holy joy to see the people tread the holy places in the fervor of an excellent devotion."[5] Such was the culmination of the First Crusade and the Christian charity manifested towards the "Infidels."

Pope Urban II never received word of the victory. Two weeks after the fall of Jerusalem, he died, uncertain whether the war he instigated would produce lasting results. For the next two centuries, subsequent popes continued the campaigns Urban initiated until the unremitting conflict was too unpalatable for the people of Europe, and the crusades had run their course.

LATER CRUSADES

Success of the First Crusade can be directly attributed to the lack of unity among the Muslims. With warring factions among various Islamic peoples, European fighters exploited this weakness and were eventually able to capture Jerusalem. Subsequent crusades, by contrast, were not as successful, because Muslims set aside their differences and came together in unity. Also absent was the element of surprise, which had worked so effectively in the initial conquest.

With the crusading spirit in full swing, nearly two-hundred thousand crusaders left for the Holy Land under the leadership of Louis VII of France and Conrad III of Germany. Constantly repelled by the Turkish army, the Second Crusade accomplished little, and by 1187, the

---

4. Ibid., 5:105.
5. Ibid.

Muslims were able to regroup under the command of Saladin, the sultan of Egypt and retake Jerusalem.

News of the defeat horrified the pope, and much of Europe, especially after the initial arduous fighting to save Jerusalem. A renewed desire for revenge permeated throughout the West, leading to the Third Crusade, the Kings' Crusade. Three sovereigns were involved in this affair: Emperor Frederick Barbarossa, Richard the Lionhearted of England, and Philip II Augustus of France. Yet, despite the overwhelming force and nobility involved in this campaign, the effort failed. Emperor Frederick drowned while attempting to cross a river, and his army scattered. Richard and Philip were successful in capturing the city of Acre, but only after two years of intense struggle. Disconcerted with the war efforts and hoping to capitalize on the political situation in Europe, Philip returned to France and attempted to usurp the lands of Richard. Richard, while on his way home, was captured and held until an exorbitant ransom was paid to set him free. Thus ended the ill-fated Third Crusade.

As costly and largely ineffective as the preceding crusades were, the Fourth Crusade was even worse for Europe. Pope Innocent III called on the army to attack Saladin at his own headquarters in Egypt. But somewhere along the way, the crusade was rerouted to Constantinople where the army provoked conflict with Christians. Ruling the day, at least for the moment, the Western soldiers founded the Latin Empire of Constantinople, setting up a Latin patriarch of Constantinople, which, theoretically, reunited the East and the West under the bishop of Rome. The Byzantines, however, would have nothing to do with it. Initially incensed at the audacious grab for power, they failed to comply with the new order and continued resisting. Eventually, in 1261, the Byzantines were able to retake the city and put an end to the ecclesiastical usurping. The end result, however, was an even deeper chasm between both branches of the church.

As troubling as these crusades were, arguably the most tragic of all was the Children's Crusade. Swept up in the religious zeal of the day, invigorated by the preaching of monks, hermits, and priests, and the promise of glory from the pope himself, the children who volunteered to fight in Muslim lands were deceived into believing a lie. Eventually, the adolescent crusaders met the fate that so many others encountered during the two centuries of warfare—slaughter and abject failure on a massive scale.

The French expedition was started by a boy named Stephen, twelve years of age. One day he claimed to have had a vision in which Christ appeared to him as a pilgrim and appealed to him to organize an army to recapture Jerusalem. Soon thereafter, he left his family, convinced he was ordained by God, and travelled the countryside telling of his vision. Soon, enthusiasm spread and other children gathered around him. Boys, girls, and even some adults rallied behind the youth, swelling his following to thirty-thousand. Led by Stephen, they reached Marseilles, located on the southeast coast of France on the Mediterranean Sea, believing the waters would part as they had for Moses and the Israelites. But alas, the waves did not obey Stephen's command as they had anticipated. Distraught at their plight but not yet ready to give up hope, Stephen and his followers found a glimmer of hope in the reassurances two men who sincerely told the young leader they believed in what the children were doing and offered safe passage to the children at no cost. Seven vessels set sail, but along the way, two vessels were shipwrecked with everyone onboard drowning just off the coast of Sardinia. The remaining ships sailed to the African shores where the rest of the children were sold into slavery.

Another crusade of children, this one led by a German boy, Nicholas, age ten, ended in a similar fate. With about two-thirds the followers of Stephen, the children set out East to fight the "infidels". One group marched through Switzerland, across the Alps; the children were never heard from again. The majority died of hunger and malnutrition, others were devoured by wild beasts, and still more fell victim to thieves and robbers. Undaunted by the dwindling force, Nicholas took a group and set sail for Genoa. When he arrived in port he discovered no ship would carry him any further. The crusaders lost the fight even before reaching the field of battle. Some, nevertheless, stayed in the city, while others returned to their homelands—dejected and discouraged that they were not given the opportunity to fight for Christ as they had been promised.

RESULTS OF THE CRUSADES

By any objective standard, the crusades failed in all three respects: to regain Jerusalem permanently, to check the advance of Muslim expansion, and to heal the schism between the East and West. By the end of two centuries of warfare, the Muslims had gained a stronghold in an expanding territory, and the rift with the East was deeper than before.

The vices and atrocities committed by "Christians" under the banner of the cross were, without question, deplorable and antithetical to the teachings of Christ. As more than one writer correctly noted in the wake of the bloodshed, many took a myopic approach and made the fatal mistake of envisioning the conquest of earthly Jerusalem the ultimate goal, forgetting about the heavenly city. The real Jerusalem is not on earth, but, regrettably, the majority did not acknowledge this crucial point.

Another lamentable reality that followed the crusades—which remains true even to this day—is the deepening contempt of Muslims towards Christians. While the memory of the crusades have all but faded from the minds of those in the West, the savagery committed by armies fighting under the banner of the Christian cross remained alive in the hearts of Muslims toward the doctrines of Christianity. Spiritual fruits failed to follow the actions of the crusades, and in so doing, the actions of the masses turned their enemies against Christianity. The deplorable actions of so many generated a perverted view of following Christ.

Aside from this poignant reality, the crusades also gave impetus for the rapid development of the system of indulgences (pardon that guarantees forgiveness of sin), which became the dogma of medieval theologians and the issue which was chiefly addressed by Martin Luther in his *95 Theses*. The question every reader should be contemplating after studying the crusades is: What could cause so many individuals to commit such horrific, barbarous actions in the name of Christ? While not always an easy answer to provide, perhaps the greatest justification for doing so was the promise of full and complete remission of sins. Though not originated by Urban II, the practice and extension of granting indulgences for sins gave cover to the many atrocities committed under the banner of "just war."

Moreover, the practice of granting religious exemption from future punishment did not end with those who fought the infidels in the East. Instead, the scope of granting indulgences was eventually broadened to include the destruction of "Christian heretics" in Western Europe as well. Indeed, indulgences were at the heart of the sacrament of penance in medieval society. Voices such as those of John Wycliffe and John Hus spoke out against the church abuses, but their beliefs were not allowed to spread broadly. Finally, a German monk had witnessed enough corruption that he took up the pen in opposition to abuses in the Roman

Church, which included the foundation of one of the three essential sacraments Rome insists is necessary for salvation.

INDULGENCES CONSIDERED IN LIGHT OF SCRIPTURE

So what exactly are indulgences, and what's the significance? Is the entire concept really that big of a deal? Simply put, indulgences are the means by which the Roman Catholic Church claims to give remission before God of the *temporal* punishment due to sins. Fundamental to the theology of indulgences is the distinction between *eternal* and *temporal* punishment. Roman theology teaches the former is removed in absolution, given by the priest, for Jesus' sake. The latter, however, can only be removed through effort and penitential acts. So it is with this second aspect that indulgences are believed to function in the church via the pope (or perhaps bishops as well). When the pope grants an indulgence to a believer, all or part of the temporal punishment due to sin is expunged.

So upon what basis does the Roman Catholic Church allege the authority to grant indulgences? Part and parcel of this doctrine is the belief in a "treasury of merit"—spiritual capital the church purportedly gained through the good works of saints, persecution, and martyrdom. The church can then draw upon this reservoir of good works for those who are in spiritual need granted at the pope's disposal in the form of an indulgence. The practice of granting indulgences, however, was soon expanded to the dead. In 1477, Pope Sixtus IV declared that indulgences were also valid for the deceased. So beginning in the fifteenth century, indulgences were sold to the populace in order to shorten their relatives in purgatory.

The Reformers, by contrast, came to see the bankruptcy of the sacramental system Rome was offering. Confession, after all, only provided solace for a short while. Yet, sins were constant and abounding. What if someone committed a sin and never realized it? That is, if sins had to be confessed in order to be forgiven, what happens to unconfessed sin? Someone must pay the punishment due for these transgressions. Who would that be?

These are just a few of the ongoing struggles many believers endured. Confronted with the reality in never being able to find peace with God in the sacramental system, many abandoned the theology that could not provide lasting hope or peace with God. Stuck on the constant treadmill of works righteousness and self-remittance of punishment, the

Reformers understood they needed more than a priest telling them their sins are forgiven—they needed an act of God that would take away all sins, past, present, and future.

Finally, after diligently seeking God's Word, the light dawned on all those who were eager to know how they could truly be right before God. A sinner is justified by faith without the works of the law. They came to understand justification is the legal declaration in which God declares the unrighteous to be not guilty, even though he remains a sinner. Paul said, "For if Abraham was justified by works, he has something to boast about, but not before God. For what does the Scripture say? Abraham believed God, and it was counted to him as righteousness" (Rom 4:2–3). The word *counted* is the same word translated elsewhere as *reckoned* or *imputed*, a legal term often used to credit money to someone else's account.

Justification is God's forensic act in which he declares all sins to be covered because of the work of Jesus Christ on the cross at Calvary (Rom 3:21–26). So it is not necessary for the sinner to recall every sin he has ever committed, because his sins have already been paid in full by Christ. When God looks upon sinners who believe in him, he sees them cloaked in the righteousness of his Son. He is fully and forever received into the kingdom. And because he is legally declared to be holy, God can make him a fellow-heir with Christ.

Of course, the Bible insists that true Christians confess their sins even after being justified (1 John 1:9). But, doing this will only restore fellowship with the Father; it is not required in order to reestablish the legal relationship with him. So when the believer is asked why he should be permitted into heaven, his answer should correspond something analogous to this: "Because I am covered in and through the righteousness of my perfect and complete Savior, Christ Jesus."

The Reformers found inexpressible joy once they no longer had to offer their pennies for Christ's riches. They did not have to continue in their efforts to stand before a holy God in their own righteousness. This discovery in the late Middle Ages was nothing new. It was the same gospel taught by Jesus and zealously defended by the apostles. But the sad fact was that it had to be rediscovered after so many years. The external church had drifted so far from the New Testament, it took a revolution to find the gospel of grace. And the system of indulgences was just one step further away from obscuring the truth of the atonement and the simplicity of salvation by grace alone through faith alone on account of Christ alone.

If only the crusaders had understood the gospel of free grace more intimately, perhaps much of the bloodshed committed in the name of Christ would have been avoided. And if professing Christians marching to the Holy Land would have rightly comprehended that true guarantee of salvation comes only from recognizing one's utter sinfulness and placing absolute faith and confidence in Jesus Christ—and not in papal declarations—the world, presumably, would never had heard the lamentable actions of medieval Christians.

Think About It

1. Why would people want to believe in a system of indulgences?
2. What do indulgences say about the atonement?
3. How would you explain the doctrine of justification to a Roman Catholic or to a non-believer?
4. Is there ever a time to wage war against non-Christians?
5. How would you respond to the taking of the Holy Land by non-Christian conquerors?

6

In Quest for Reformation

(1305–1516)

THE ZENITH OF PAPAL power was achieved during the thirteenth century under the leadership of Innocent III (*c.* 1160–1216). It was during this time period that crusaders recaptured Constantinople, seemingly healing the schism. Universities thrived, developing theological systems from Aristotelian philosophy; massive buildings were erected in which the enormous stones forming the style known as Gothic art overcame ostensible natural limitations; and mendicant orders were established to win converts to Christ through proselytizing.

More importantly, however, Europe was united under a spiritual head, the so-called Vicar of Christ, who uttered infallible and inerrant truths in matters of faith and practice when speaking from the chair of Peter. For this reason, no source outside the church could stand over her, correcting and reforming her when she departed from the truth. By degree and over the course of centuries, error permeated the church's teaching, yielding disastrous results.

Because many denizens of Europe came to view the pope as the universal head of the church and myopically gave their allegiance to him, the office of Roman bishop became a political position that believer and unbeliever alike desired. After years of gross mismanagement, simony, and exploiting the fears of a superstitious public, the dawn of the fourteenth century witnessed a church that in many respects was no longer catholic in geography, evangelical in belief, or gospel-oriented in theology. Originally founded upon the apostles with Jesus as the cornerstone, the Catholic Church had gradually evolved into the monarchial episcopate of the papacy.

How was this universal headship in the West accomplished? The answer to that question is not always simple, for there were many contributing factors that culminated in the development of the office of the papacy. A good starting point in understanding the rise of the Roman Church is the realization it was the only church in the West which claimed apostolic origin. Early tradition credits Peter and Paul as having established the church, with later belief dropping Paul and crediting it solely to Peter.

Other contributing aspects include Constantine's relocation of the capital of the empire to Constantinople (thus leaving a political void for the bishop to fill), forged Decretals purportedly giving jurisdiction and power to the bishop of Rome,[1] political maneuverings and alliances, the purchase of vast amounts of land, an illiterate and uneducated public, and retained elements of Gnostic influence.[2] All of these factors, and more, combined until the Roman Catholic Church became the dominant political and religious institution throughout Europe.

In so doing, there were some inevitable and harmful repercussions. Simony and concupiscence characterized all levels of the hierarchy with priests—and even a few popes—living in open debauchery and subjecting the papacy to the greatest indignities. Some popes possessed ruthlessness and an insatiable appetite for absolute power, bringing profound disrepute, intrigue, and debauchery to the office. Popes led armies into brutal conflict based on greed, made war on political dissenters, conspired and betrayed leaders for power, and armed themselves with the tool of assassinations, while others openly took concubines and fathered children.

So great, indeed, was the corruption of this period that later generations referred to the Roman Church during the first half of the tenth century as the "Pornocracy" or the "Rule of the Harlots," leading many

---

1. The Pseudo-Isadorian Decretals are a collection of falsified documents seeming to support the bishop of Rome's claim to authority and jurisdiction over the universal church. However, discoveries in the fifteenth century confirmed the suspicion that these were, indeed, spurious documents. Ironically, though the foundation of papal authority has been dismantled, the dogma of papal infallibility has since been decreed. Not only this, a large portion of Roman Canon Law, still in existence today, is based upon these forged documents.

2. For instance, the first reference to the Assumption of Mary is found in the fifth century apocryphal gospel known as the *Transitus Beatae Mariae*, which was spuriously attributed to Melito of Sardis. But more than this, beliefs such as the Assumption—originating with Gnostic thought—slowly gained a stronghold and formed the basis for a number of unbiblical doctrines.

under her influence to question her practices, and others concluded the pope was the biblical anti-Christ.[3]

Beginning in 1305, Pope Clement V, a Frenchman, moved to France from Rome and then to Avignon in 1309. The papacy remained there until 1377 when it returned to the imperial city, thus ending the "Babylonian Captivity." Clement, a man of weak character, little experience, and poor health, was a tool in the hand of the civil authorities. Compelled by the French king to satisfy his own personal ambitions, Clement proved to be an ineffective leader from his office. Yet, what is interesting to note about his reign is that his pontificate marked the end of the official medieval collections of canon law, the body of ecclesiastical legislation that encompasses all domains of church life. Clement's troubling reign, therefore, marks the period from which reform was, arguably, most necessary.

What had not ceased, and in fact only increased, were the manifest abuses remaining within the external church. Against this unfortunate backdrop, many reformers within the established church and throughout her history did not set out to form new denominations, break with heritage, or even create schism. Rather, zealous supporters desired to reform the church from within, correcting her of abuses that had slowly crept in over time.

Disconcerted with the increasing moral and theological corruption, calls for reform were made. John Wycliffe, John Huss, and Girolamo Savaronola were three such individuals who sounded the clarion call for returning to the simplicity of the early church. These champions of truth endeavored to bring her out of the mire into which she had sunk.

Much to the chagrin of the modern day Roman Catholic Church, we would do well here to point out that accomplishing this necessary reform presupposes the idea that popes and councils are not infallible and can, in fact, follow after error. Indeed, the only way for one to determine reforms are necessary at all is to admit, at least tacitly, that the teaching magisterium has, to some degree, violated biblical standards. And that belief is precisely what drove Christian believers during the Middle Ages to protest overtly. Only after the teachings of the church were compared with sacred Scripture were they able to recognize many aspects were incompatible with the plain teaching of Holy Writ. What they ultimately discovered was that some doctrines had departed from scriptural moorings.

---

3. See Chamberlin, *The Bad Popes*.

Instead of gratitude, the reformers were met with rigid disapproval. For attempting to bring about revival, these early reformers were attacked unmercifully, often at the expense of life. The Roman Catholic behemoth suppressed dissent and, as we shall see, asserted its own hegemony over those who failed to follow the teachings of the magisterium unconditionally.

JOHN WYCLIFFE

Heralded as the "Morning Star of the Reformation," John Wycliffe, an Englishman, lived during the Avignon papacy. Born in 1324 in the village of Wyclif, Yorkshire, in the diocese of Durham,[4] Wycliffe is often said to have anticipated the teachings of Luther. That is, he was a doctrinal reformer, writing copiously against ecclesiastical abuses and firmly believing every person should read the Bible in his own native tongue. To this end, he dedicated his life and made it his chief aim to correct error that infiltrated the church, thus championing theological and practical reform.

Wycliffe's early life has, so far as is known, been lost to history. Most of his career was spent at Oxford where he became renowned for his breadth of knowledge and unassailable logic. Finally, in 1371, during the papacy's rule in Avignon, Wycliffe left the university to serve the crown, initially as a diplomat, and then as a polemicist against French interests. In so doing, he argued for limitations on any institution, whether it is secular or religious, and taught dominion should be characterized by the example of Christ. Even legitimate institutions, he argued, should not overstep their boundaries beyond what God has established.

Constant quarreling ensued over the question of the legitimacy of papal taxation and temporal authority of the Roman bishop. Forced assessments and annual payments to Rome seemed, to Wycliffe, to be an overreach of authority. Even the ecclesiastical domain, he thought, must be subject to limitations, as well as the scope of civil power.

During this same time period, the Western Schism[5] in the church began, legitimizing Wycliffe's convictions regarding ecclesiastical usur-

---

4. Like many figures of history, the precise date and location of Wycliffe's birth is not always agreed upon. Some scholars prefer a date of 1330 and a location of Hipswell, half a mile from Wyclif. More than this, Wycliffe's name is spelled more than twenty different ways. The earliest mention of the name in any official document, dated July 26, 1374, gives it Wiclif.

5. The Western Schism, beginning in 1378, refers to the period in which the Western

pation. The scandal emboldened his protests, and he began teaching the true church is not merely the pope and bishops, but rather, the entirety of all true believers—those whom God elected for salvation, just has Augustine had taught centuries earlier. Since there was no way to tell who comprised the elect, the fruits that each person produced manifested the reality of their belonging to the true church or not. And since many within the hierarchy of the Roman Church produced no visible fruit so far as he could tell, Wycliffe doubted their spiritual standing. Later in life, Wycliffe even went so far as to conclude the pope himself fell outside the scope of genuine Christianity.

As controversial as attacking the spiritual condition of members of the Roman Church was, it was not until his public repudiation of transubstantiation that he truly aroused the indignation of the magisterium. First established as dogma at the Fourth Lateran Council in 1215, Wycliffe denied the church's teaching that the blood and wine blessed during the Eucharist miraculously transformed into the actual body and blood of Christ. Responding to the doctrine, he penned a list of theses in which he argued in great specificity why the doctrine was unscriptural. It was the first time in nearly the century and a half since the dogmatic teaching became official that someone challenged its veracity in such a public manner. Just as Athanasius did in the fourth century (even against the bishop of Rome), Wycliffe seemingly stood alone in his dissent of the egregious doctrinal error.

Needless to say, since Wycliffe's proclamations stood at open variance with official doctrine, his views were condemned as heretical and unorthodox, although he was never formally condemned by name. Convinced the judges failed to refute his theses satisfactorily, Wycliffe returned to Oxford where he continued preaching and teaching. There, he enjoyed an almost unprecedented status of immunity for the reputation and prestige he garnered earlier as an erudite and theological scholar. For the next several years he continued lecturing, studying, and writing in relative peace.

---

branch of Christendom had three lines of popes, with the entire continent of Europe falling under the anathema of a rival pope. It was not until the Council of Constance elected Martin V that the schism finally abated. Ironically, the Council of Constance concluded that even the pope himself was bound to obey councils in matters of faith and practice, yet, Martin V, the very pope elected by the council, declared his superiority to all councils.

In the year 1381, Wycliffe retired to his parish in Lutterworth. It was here that he made his pioneering translation of the Bible into the English language. According to Wycliffe, the Scriptures rightly belong in the hands of every believer. Christians, no matter how learned or simple, deserve the Word of God in their own tongue. After all, every individual functions under divine command to obey the law of God so it is only appropriate that all persons are able to read for themselves what those commands are. Moreover, Wycliffe completed what was considered by many to be his most important—and arguably most influential—treatise, the *Trialogus*, during the final years at his parish. In it, he set forth the principle that, where Scripture and the pope differ, the former is to be followed, and, where civil authorities and the conscience are at open variance, the latter is to be obeyed. So in that spirit and to that end, Wycliffe spent the remainder of his life translating the Latin Vulgate into the English language.

Before Wycliffe finished his *magnum opus*, the English New Testament, he was struck with paralysis while attending a church service. A few days later, Wycliffe finally passed into eternity on December 31, 1384, "having lit a fire which shall never be put out,"[6] as one historian rightly put it.

Because Wycliffe openly opposed the established hierarchy, advocated jurisdictional and spiritual limitations, and opposed moral and theological abuses in the church, he was branded a heretic. One chronicler recorded the prevailing sentiment of his life:

> "On the feast of the passion of St. Thomas of Canterbury, John de Wyclif, that instrument of the devil, that enemy of the Church, that author of confusion to the common people, that image of hypocrites, that idol of heretics, that author of schism, that sower of hatred, that coiner of lies, being struck with the horrible judgment of God, was smitten with palsy and continued to live till St. Silvester's Day, on which he breathed out his malicious spirit into the abodes of darkness."[7]

The years following his demise were equally disheartening. By decree, his writings were suppressed and his books burned. The Council of Constance (1415) condemned Wycliffe formally and ordered his body

---

6. Schaff, 3:149.
7. Ibid.

to be exhumed so that his corpse could be turned to ashes. His remains were then cast into the river Swift.

Wycliffe, sadly, was not the only person to fall victim to the Council of Constance. We will next be introduced to another vocal critic who met a fatal end for his so-called aberrant views, questioning the authority of the established Roman Church.

JOHN HUSS

While Wycliffe preached reform on the island of Britain, across the continent in Bohemia (present day Czech Republic), another reformist movement was taking shape. Similar to the spiritual progress underway in Britain, the religious fervor in Bohemia could not be suppressed. The leader of this famous movement, John Huss, was born into humble beginnings in 1374. From early on, his calling was certain; he was destined for the priesthood and academics. Huss served in both the church and the university. Ordained as a priest in 1401, his scholarly inclinations led him to become the rector of the University of Prague only a year later. From his lofty position in academia and from the pulpit at the Bethlehem Chapel, he advocated substantial change within the ecclesiastical realm. Not yet ready to make calls for widespread theological reform, Huss, at first, only persisted in wanting to restore integrity to the church and in particular, the life of the clergy.

Huss championed these causes, because he was greatly influenced by Wycliffe's teachings. Even though many of Wycliffe's writings were originally burned, select works managed to survive and made their way into Huss' native Bohemia. Since the printing press would not be invented for several more decades, Huss painstakingly copied Wycliffe's books for his own personal use. The Bohemian preacher emphasized personal piety, devotion, and purity in life. More importantly still, he emphasized the centrality of the Bible in the service. Because of his strong stance, he stressed exegetical sermons in the chapel services. Eventually what he discovered from deep examinations of the Scripture was the ignominious nature of Christ's life and the example he set to be followed.

Huss' newfound love for simplicity, as demonstrated in the life of Christ and the apostles, was displayed tangibly in the chapel. Hanging on the walls were paintings, contrasting biblical images of Christ's service with the ostentatious and pompous display of the pope. One such portrait showed people kissing the feet of the bishop of Rome, juxtaposed with Jesus washing the feet of his disciples. Another pictured the pope riding a horse with his entourage, while Jesus walked barefoot and solemn on the dusty roads. Even to the uneducated and illiterate, the message was clear: The extravagant display that now characterized the Roman Church was in need of restoration.

In 1409, the Council of Pisa was convoked to end the Western Schism by deposing two rival popes. Instead of ending the discord, however, a third papal claimant was elected, and now there were three popes, all claiming apostolic succession. This manifest absurdity only served to crystallize in Huss' mind the outrageous claims of papal pretensions. Rome's organizational chaos—combined with an order from the archbishop of Prague telling Huss to stop preaching and ordering the university to burn Wycliffe's writings—gave impetus for the Bohemian preacher to reflect seriously upon his own beliefs. In so doing, Huss determined he could not obey the order and refused to burn Wycliffe's writings.

Accordingly, he was summoned to Rome to answer for his obstinacy and for all those who followed him in his ways. Again, he refused and was excommunicated in 1411, with the city of Prague formally being placed under an interdict—meaning, no one in the city could receive the sacraments. Even though Huss had the support of the people and the king, he left the city to become an itinerant preacher, traveling the country and speaking to all who would gladly hear him.

The controversy with the papacy led Huss to contemplate the entire institution and its theological foundation, after which, he adopted more radical views. First, he came to the conclusion that unworthy popes did not have to be obeyed when they acted according to their own selfish ambitions and not for the general welfare of the church. Second, and perhaps most notably, this drove him to the logical conclusion that the Bible alone is the final authority by which popes and believers are to be judged. After all, if the pope stands in clear violation of Scripture, why should anyone be obliged to listen to him?

In addition to rejecting papal claims of universal authority, he denounced the manifest immoral and profligate lifestyle that characterized so many of the clergy, including the popes themselves. Also, he wrote a book in which he argued that God alone can forgive sins and not the clergy. Because Huss was so influential, the hierarchy of the church acted swiftly in opposing him. After all, his point of view, if widely held, would disrupt the fabric of the magisterium and threaten her hegemony over Christian believers.

With profound opposition to the current state of affairs and harboring deep-seated antipathy to the corruption within, when Huss received the news that a general council was to be held at Constance—and that the Emperor invited him there with the promise of safe-conduct to attend—it was no wonder he accepted the invitation. Unbeknownst to him, however, upon arriving in Constance, he was taken into the papal consistory and ordered to recant of his "heresies". Huss responded that he would joyfully repent of his errors if someone could show him from Scripture and reason where he erred. But no one would. The authorities refused to engage him in debate. Instead, in response to his stubborn position, Huss was arrested and treated as a prisoner. The emperor, not wanting to be seen as taking the side of a heretic, acquiesced without keeping his promise.

On June 5, 1415, Huss was taken before the council, while still in chains, to answer charges of heresy. The authorities insisted he recant of his false doctrines, but for Huss to admit he was wrong would be to acknowledge that he and all his friends and followers were heretics. Though sick and physically wasting away from the debilitating effects of imprisonment and maltreatment, he refused to renounce his alleged errors unless he could be shown he was wrong from the Scriptures, saying he would not "recede from the truth." Again, the council refused to discuss any theological issues with Huss and ordered him back to his cell to await his ultimate fate.

Finally, a month later on July 6, 1415, Huss, dressed in priestly garments as a form of mockery, was escorted one final time from his cell in the cathedral. Somewhere along the way, his robes were torn from his fragile body, his head shaved, and he was forced to wear a paper crown adorned with pictures of demons. Walking the path to the site of his impending execution, he passed by a churchyard in which a pile of his books were being burned—a foreshadowing of what was to come.

After arriving at the designated area and being tied to a stake, he was given one last opportunity to recant. And once again, he refused to capitulate to the authorities. Moved to prayer at that moment, he uttered the words: "Lord Jesus, it is for thee that I patiently endure this cruel death. I pray thee to have mercy on my enemies."[8] As the fire was lighted and the flames licked at his weakened body, he was heard reciting the

---

8. Gonzalez, *The Story of Christianity: The Early Church to the Dawn of the Reformation*.

Psalms. Those were the final words Huss would audibly and clearly speak. No shouts of condemnation for his persecutors; no harsh words of ire directed toward the ecclesiastical rulers. Instead, words of mercy and praise sprang forth from his lips.

Only a few days afterward, Huss' friend, Jerome of Prague, decided to join him at Constance. It proved to be a fatal mistake. Venturing to the city cost Jerome his life as well. The ashes of both men were gathered by the executioners and dispersed into a nearby lake so that their bodies and gravesites would not become a memorial place.

When news reached the Bohemians of what transpired at Constance, the people were indignant, with some calling for action against the council. The masses were outraged. Despite being forbidden to do so, Huss' followers came together in his memory to honor his sacrifice. In all, four hundred and fifty-two noblemen assembled to pay homage to Huss and to reaffirm the general consensus that an unworthy pope ought not to be obeyed. And the unjust execution was just more confirmation of this mounting belief.

Huss' tragic death only increased his prestige among the people. His followers subsequently came out in overt rebellion to the Roman Catholic Church and to the German-dominated empire, neither of which wanted to contest the Hussites. Though the church officially tried to stamp out the dissenters, Huss' followers swelled in number. A large fraction left the established church and formed the *Unitas Fratrum*, Union of Brethren. Not only did the movement grow in Bohemia, but it stretched to nearby Moravia. The movement survived the moment and, during the Protestant Reformation of the sixteenth century, the Brethren eventually morphed into a larger group of believers more commonly called "Moravians."

GIROLAMO SAVONAROLA

Though an obscure and oftentimes forgotten figure in the history of the church, Girolamo Savonarola remains arguably one of the greatest reformers, teachers, preachers, politicians, and philosophers Christianity has produced. Embarking on a public career as a preacher in the same year Martin Luther was born, Savonarola would have unquestioningly been the prominent figure in ushering in the Protestant Reformation had Italy been more congenial to reform. As it was, Savonarola stands as the precursor to the sixteenth-century movement. So vocal was he in denouncing the established church that Luther later spoke highly of the Italian preacher and referred to him as a "Protestant martyr". Not only was Savonarola instrumental in bringing much-needed change to a corrupt institution, but he was also successful in rescuing many from the skepticism that flooded the continent after so many were disillusioned by a corrupt church. Thanks to his powerful oratory skills, deep philosophizing, and commitment to living an upright lifestyle, he was able to convince the masses that religion was not all a sham.

A native of Ferrara, Savonarola was intended by his family to enter into the medical profession, but a refusal of marriage in his youth facilitated a new direction. Instead, he entered into a life of monasticism. Initially beginning as a Dominican in 1474 in the city of Bologna, he was later transferred to St. Mark in Florence in the year 1482, where, only nine years later, he was elected prior. While at St. Mark, he began teaching his fellow friars, expounding Scripture with great clarity and persuasion.

Soon, his reputation as a skilled orator and profound theologian garnered him enough attention that the lessons were moved from the garden to the church in order to accommodate the growing crowd. By the time of Lent in 1491, his popularity had increased so greatly that he was invited to preach in the main church in Florence. There, he waxed eloquent in calling sinners to repentance and conversion and warned of impending trials and tribulations.

Indeed, his messages were timely and his warnings seemed prophetic. The French invaded in 1494, which appeared to confirm Savonarola's status as a divine spokesman. The subsequent overthrow of the Medici family—who practically owned most of Florence—made him the *de facto* ruler. Acting as its authoritative leader, he set out to reform the city and to turn Florence into a penitential city. So he embarked on some unpopular tasks. Namely, he sold the church's vast quantities of gold and silver and gave the proceeds to the poor. He further forbade the much popular carnival, because he viewed it as the epitome of profligacy, and also burned all "vanities"—cards, dice, jewelry, dresses, wigs, cosmetics, and others alike.

During these years of purging, Savonarola's message also changed. Instead of the apocalyptic, doomsday sermons, he spoke words of encouragement and hope and preached optimistic messages of Florence morphing into the "city of God." So in the spirit of continual reform, it was also during this time period that Savonarola attempted to bring credibility to the monasteries, attempting to eradicate the impression that monks tended to be uneducated and fanatical. So for this reason, friars at St. Mark's studied the biblical languages, as well as Latin and Chaldean. Moral revolution and academic change were integrally linked in a progression toward the city for which Savaronola longed.

But all was not well in Florence. Proponents of the deposed Medici despised Savaronola for his political fortunes. More importantly, though, Savaronola made an unfortunate alliance with France and against Pope Alexander VI. In response, the pope issued a series of draconian measures, first against Savaronola and then against the city. In addition to being excommunicated, the inhabitants of the city were losing a great deal of money from the trade restrictions, and the wealthy and influential began to turn against him. Savaronola's followers demanded he perform miracles to demonstrate his divine calling, but when he failed to produce sufficient evidence, they, too, turned against their leader.

Finally, after an extensive period of plotting against Savaronola, a mob formed and stormed the monastery of St. Mark where he was residing. Refusing to defend himself or allow anyone to take up arms in his defense, he was seized by the tumultuous crowd, bound and beaten, and turned over to the civil authorities.

Unable to muster any credible charges against Savaronola—and after several weeks of physical abuse and general deprivations by his tormentors—papal legates and other dissenters involved in the judicial process formally accused him and two of his friends of being "heretics and schismatics," though the exact nature of the heresy was never defined. Being convicted of these "crimes," the ecclesiastical authorities turned Savaronola and several supporters over to the civil authorities to be executed. If ever there was any mercy in their method of execution, it was only that each was hanged before being burned to ashes. Afterwards, the remains were thrown into the river Arno in hopes that their memory would be lost to future generations. Such would not be the case, however, as Savaronola's quest for reform lived on and was fulfilled in only a matter of decades in the distant region of Germany.

THE MEASURING ROD FOR EVERY BELIEVER

The one recurring pattern throughout the history of the redemptive process of God's people is that reformation took shape only after the hearing or reading of God's commands. From the rediscovery of the Book of the Law by Hilkiah in the Old Testament to the many reformers who recognized the external church had strayed from the simplicity of the written Word, only after people were subjected to an ultimate, unchanging authority did they realize something was amiss.

Indeed, the Word of God is *the* standard by which all norms are to be evaluated, since it functions as the only measuring rod (because of its nature—"God-breathed") by which faith and practice are to be judged. Otherwise, when there is no official standard standing above the church, guiding and correcting her when she strays, she will only continue in her perverse ways as history has amply demonstrated.

When the church places herself above the Word, functioning as the only institution that has the right to interpret the Word, theological disaster ensues. The question every Christian must therefore ask is: "Are we led to believe from the Bible itself that someone else other than the person of God has the sole right and duty to determine the meaning of Scripture?" Even though the thrust of this topic was touched upon in chapter one, the significance of this topic bears repeating, and the entirety of this doctrine must be understood properly and thoroughly by any lover of truth.

The first church historian, Luke, gives us a clear indication in his Gospel his purpose for writing:

> "Inasmuch as many have undertaken to compile a narrative of the things that have been accomplished among us, just as those who from the beginning were eyewitnesses and ministers of the word have delivered them to us, it seemed good to me also, having followed all things closely for some time past, to write an orderly account for you, most excellent Theophilus, *that you may have certainty concerning the things you have been taught*" (Luke 1:1–4, emphasis mine).

Luke's primary reason for writing to Theophilus, as he indicates, was to provide him with an absolute certainty of the things he had already been taught. Luke here gives us no indication that his words are unknowable or that Theophilus needed an infallible magisterium in order to understand what Luke intended. If it were necessary, the thorough and exacting Luke would certainly have prescribed it, as would other New Testament writers.

Likewise, Paul expresses this same supposition, that is, his readers would understand his own words when he said, "But even if we or an angel from heaven should preach to you a gospel contrary to the one we preached to you, let him be accursed" (Gal 1:8). The indication here is, of course, that Paul's audience would use their own judgment to determine if any given message they might hear was, in fact, consistent with the purity of the gospel message or if it was an aberration from the truth.

Paul did not call on his readers to submit to an infallible teaching magisterium. Instead, he commanded them to exercise their ability to discern truth from error by comparing what they would have obviously already received, understood, and vouchsafed in their minds as the true and pure gospel along with their ability to compare a message to the rest of Scripture. All of this is consistent with the evangelical doctrine that Scripture is perspicuous.

With this understanding in mind, let us now turn our attention to the question of what the Bible actually teaches concerning this matter. Does the Bible specifically teach its own sufficiency? Some groups, unquestionably, deny this very point. I once encountered a man who tried to convince me that no one in the early church believed in the sufficiency of Scripture. He persisted in arguing the first historical documentation of anyone publicly advocating the principle of *sola Scripture* was none other than Martin Luther at the Synod of Augsburg in 1518. No one prior to this, he insisted, believed in this doctrine.

Sadly, his comment is all too representative of the shallow understanding of church history that is ubiquitous in our day—and that includes professing believers on both sides of the aisle. Bruce Shelley often told the story of how he displayed a particular *Peanuts* strip on the door of his study to encourage easy conversation for any student who stopped by his office. This one comic strip dealt with Charlie Brown's little sister Sally who was writing a theme for school entitled, "Church History." Charlie, looking over her shoulder, notices her opening comments, "When writing about church history, we have to go back to the very beginning. Our pastor was born in 1930." Charlie shakes his head and rolls his eyes upward.

Far too many Christians suffer from this same general lack of awareness about the past. The time between Pentecost and the present is mostly a fog. And this is not what God has in mind or wants from us. I do wish more people would take this topic seriously and understand their roots—but I digress. Returning to the point of discussion, it was hard for me to believe this man had any familiarity with the teachings of Jesus, Athanasius, Wycliffe, Huss, or any other number of believers who would have, without reservation, disagreed with his conclusion. Let me briefly point out a few examples, first beginning with the apostle Paul.

The primary passage most frequently cited in support of using the Bible alone is found in Paul's second letter to Timothy. Oftentimes dismissed without adequate reason, many Roman Catholics insist Protestants cannot muster a single verse in support of the Reformation principle. But is this true? Let's investigate this allegation.

Writing shortly before his impending demise, Paul wrote these final words of exhortation to his fellow laborer in Christ:

> "But as for you, continue in what you have learned and have firmly believed, knowing from whom you learned it and how from childhood you have been acquainted with the sacred writings, which are able to make you wise for salvation through faith in Christ Jesus. All Scripture is breathed out by God and profitable for teaching, for reproof, for correction, and for training in righteousness, that the man of God may be competent, equipped for every good work" (2 Tim 3:14–17).

I believe it is only proper to begin by noting, once again, the nature of Scripture. That is, Scripture is *theopneustos*, literally "God-breathed." Because of its divine source, the God-breathed Scriptures cannot, by definition, have any greater authority. Considered by many to have proffered the greatest exegesis of this word, B. B. Warfield's exhaustive treatment of pointing out the profound significance of originating from the mouth of God remains without equal. Summing up his treatise, then, Warfield concluded (along with many others) that which is ultimately *theopneustos* can have no higher authority, because there can be no greater authority than the very words of God. And what did Paul say was God-breathed? "All Scripture."

It is sometimes at this point that Roman Catholic apologists try to point out an error in evangelical thinking. Following the mistake of Cardinal Newman, some modern day Roman Catholic apologists say that if this verse proves the sufficiency of Scripture, then it proves too much. How so? Well, they insist Paul is here speaking only of the Old Testament. If true, they continue, this would render the New Testament superfluous.

Answering this objection should be accomplished by noting two important points. First, Timothy had in his possession more than just the Old Testament. When the second letter was written to him, he would have had available to him, not only the entire corpus of Paul's writings (since the second epistle to Timothy was Paul's final letter) but several Gospels as well. 1 Timothy 5:17–18 reads, "Let the elders who rule well be considered worthy of double honor, especially those who labor in preaching and teaching. For the Scripture says, 'You shall not muzzle an ox when it treads out the grain,' and, 'The laborer deserves his wages.'" Why is this significant? Paul writes, "For the Scriptures says," and then follows with a quote from Deuteronomy, followed by a verse from Luke 10:7 and Matthew 10:10.

So it becomes clearer, then, by the time Timothy received the second epistle from Paul, he had, at a minimum, twelve other Pauline letters in addition to at least two other Gospel accounts (and perhaps the Gospel of Mark as well if most scholars date the book appropriately).

Second, and more importantly, Paul's point is not to imply Timothy doesn't need additional Scripture or that further revelation was not forthcoming. Instead, what the apostle is indicating, starting in verse sixteen, is that all Scripture is breathed out by God. That is, Paul is addressing the very nature of the Bible and is not referring to the scope of the canon. Since the Bible represents God speaking, it is profitable in the Christian's life and for the work of the ministry.

When Paul delivers these final words of encouragement, he is telling him that he is not without divine assistance. God has not left the church unattended but has provided for her the Word of God. Thus, Paul is stating that all which is *theopneustos* will prove profitable for training in righteousness so that the person of God may be fully equipped, complete for every good work. And all of this is derived, not from the unwritten, vacillating tradition of men but from the Bible alone.

I pause here just long enough to point out that Paul asserts the person of God *can be* (indicating possibility) complete and fully equipped because of the availability of Scripture. Paul could have easily guided Timothy to another source or rule of faith that could prove just as useful or beneficial in his ministry, yet he does not. Why? The answer is simple if we let the Scriptures speak plainly. Because there is nothing else that is equal to or greater than that which is ultimately God-breathed. By its very definition, no rule for living can equal or surpass that which is *theopneustos*.

There was no other rule of faith that was necessary for Paul, Timothy, the early church, the medieval church, or the church today. Scripture and Scripture alone is the only rule of faith God has given to his people.

So what have we discovered thus far? First, Paul taught Timothy there is a rule of faith that is God-breathed. Because of the nature of this rule, there can be nothing higher. Second, Paul instructed Timothy in the completeness of Scripture to function in the church. That is, it was sufficient for its intended purpose of functioning as a rule of faith. And finally, Paul only refers us to this rule of faith, namely, all of Scripture, and to none other. Clearly, then, I submit *sola Scriptura* is taught plainly in the Bible.

Some might still be thinking: Is this the only verse that teaches this principle? No, definitely not. The sufficiency of Scripture is taught elsewhere, although probably not as explicitly as revealed in Second Timothy. In Matthew's Gospel, for instance, Jesus expressly indicates the sufficiency and clarity of Scriptures when responding to the Jewish leaders who attempted to condemn the apostles for breaking the tradition of the elders.

> "Then Pharisees and scribes came to Jesus from Jerusalem and said, 'Why do your disciples break the tradition of the elders? For they do not wash their hands when they eat.' He answered them, 'And why do you break the commandment of God for the sake of your tradition? For God commanded, 'Honor your father and your mother,' and, 'Whoever reviles father or mother must surely die.' But you say, 'If anyone tells his father or his mother, 'What you would have gained from me is given to God,' he need not honor his father.' So for the sake of your tradition you have made void the word of God. You hypocrites! Well did Isaiah prophesy of you, when he said: 'This people honors me with their lips, but their heart is far from me; in vain do they worship me, teaching as doctrines the commandments of men'" (Matt 15:1-9).

Ironically, Jesus is dealing with the exact issue evangelicals deal with when confronting any theological system that advocates an infallible authority or appeals to some indefinable tradition. Specifically in this situation, the Jewish leaders objected to the apostle's disregard of the extra-biblical hand washing rituals. From the Pharisees and scribes' perspective, the disciples were acting insolently by refusing to accept their authority. Moreover, they even went so far as to identify this particular ceremony as a "tradition of the elders."

Even though the cleansing practice was not contained in the Word of God, the Jewish leaders believed their man-made traditions were on par with sacred Scripture. Yet, how does Jesus respond? Does he simply bow to the alleged authority of the Jewish leaders? No. Instead, he goes on the offensive and criticizes these leaders by pointing out how they break the commandment of God for the sake of their tradition and make "void the word of God"—a stunning rebuke indeed. Jesus critiques another tradition of the elders, namely, the Korban rule,[9] compares it with God-breathed Scripture and finds it does not comport with the Word.

Granted, Jesus is not here condemning all tradition, but neither do proponents of *sola Scriptura*. In fact, we love tradition. However, all we ask for is that believers emulate Jesus by holding up any and all traditions and examining them in light of the Word, comparing them to that which is *theopneustos*.

Furthermore, it must be clearly demonstrated that traditions outside of Scripture are God-breathed if they are to be embraced as equally binding—a near impossible task outside of divine revelation. So if tradition cannot be shown to be of equal standing with the rest of God's Word, then it does not and cannot constitute or serve as a rule of faith for the church since, after all, its origin is not divine. Remember, all Scripture is breathed out by God. Therefore, unless tradition is also *theopneustos* it cannot be equal to the rest of the Word of God. For there can only be one ultimate authority, and that is why the evangelical's supreme authority is, without question or reservation, the God-breathed Scriptures and nothing more.

Think About It

1. What convinced believers in the pre-Reformation church that corruption was apparent in both doctrine and practice?
2. How can you be certain you are correctly interpreting the Bible?
3. Can you explain the sufficiency of Scripture?
4. Are traditions bad? What traditions are good? What traditions are not good? Why?
5. Is the nature of tradition and the Bible the same?

---

9. The Korban rule to which Jesus referred, and subsequently condemned, was the custom among the Pharisees of avoiding their responsibility to see to the financial need of their parents. In so doing, the Pharisees were guilty of violating the command to honor one's father and mother.

7

The Protestant Reformation

(1517–1648)

Since its inception, the greatest and most profound revolution in the established church occurred during the first half of the sixteenth century, occurring in two phases—the Protestant Reformation and then the Catholic Reformation. Both sought to cleanse the church of abuses and to bring it closer to the ideal Christian church founded by Christ, but they differed as to how this was to be accomplished.

The Catholic Reformation maintained reform was to be achieved within the existing framework of the Western tradition of Christianity, the Roman Catholic Church. It called for a moral transformation of both laity and clergy. It sought to bring a deeper understanding and appreciation for the established teachings, to cultivate spiritual life through prayer, to encourage others through service and charitable works, and to foster evangelism by fulfilling the Great Commission.

Yet, in so doing, it would avoid changes in doctrine, but would seek to clarify or to make more precise the teachings that had, presumably, always been taught and believed by all faithful Christians throughout the ages. This Catholic spirit of reform firmly believed in the unbreakable communion between the bishop of Rome (the pope) and the apostles. More importantly, however, doctrinal control over the masses was preserved through the sacraments of the Roman Church. After all, the grace of God was still channeled through the hierarchy of the church, and because of that, the sacraments were treasured by those participants.

In marked contrast, Protestants broke with the Roman Catholic Church and created the Lutheran, Anabaptist, and Reformed aspects of the Christian faith. Protestants all rejected the authoritative claims of the bishop of Rome, the subordinated role of Scripture, and all seven sacramental channels of grace as the established church insisted. For these reasons, among others, the Protestant reaction against Rome continued to swell. Movements of reform in previous generations were never stamped out. Their teachings continued to foster dissent from what many believed to be egregious, unbiblical doctrines.

Having the groundwork already laid, the moment was ripe for a German monk to question the status quo of the Roman Church. Desperately seeking a satisfactory answer to life's most important question, he asked himself: "What must I do to be right before God?" In answering that fundamental inquiry, what he discovered turned all of Europe—and the rest of the world—upside down.

MARTIN LUTHER, A TORTURED SOUL

If you were to find yourself in any of the participating German states on October 31 of any given year, you would discover that most places of business are closed in observance of Reformation Day. The public holiday celebrated in Germany commemorates the act by Martin Luther, when, on October 31, 1517, he nailed his *95 Theses* in the Latin language to the door of the Castle church in Wittenberg, soliciting scholarly debate. In so doing, Luther was not denying the veracity of indulgences *per se*, but rather, he was writing against the abuse of vendors, namely, the Dominican, John Tetzel, who manipulated the masses through the selling of indulgences for impious gain.

Tetzel became infamous for coercing many ignorant and unsuspecting denizens into purchasing documents guaranteeing remission of sin by using demagogic phrases such as, "Pity us, pity us. We are in dire torment from which you can redeem us for a pittance." And, "As soon as the coin in the coffer rings, the soul from purgatory springs."

For Luther, there were three main issues standing against Tetzel and the selling of indulgences. The late Reformation scholar Roland Bainton explains Luther's *Theses* as focusing on three main points: "an objection to the avowed object of the expenditure, a denial of the powers of the pope over purgatory, and a consideration of the welfare of the sinner."[1] Thus, it is apparent from Luther's own writing that at the time of post-

---

1. Bainton, *Here I Stand: A Life of Martin Luther*, 60–61.

ing the *Theses* his chief concern was the abuse of indulgences and not necessarily the concept thereof.

Anyone looking to Luther's document hoping to find any of the Protestant tenets might be disappointed. There is nothing particularly reformed in his *Theses*. There is no mention of the doctrine of justification, no discussion of the imputation of Christ's righteousness, no language commenting on the doctrines of grace, nor is there any indication of the idea of *sola Scriptura*—all of those biblical concepts had yet to fully germinate in the mind of Luther. It would take time before Luther came to realize that the entire system of indulgences was antithetical to Scriptures. Eventually, he wrote condemningly of the system he once naturally embraced: "Indulgences are not a pious fraud, but an infernal, diabolical, antichristian fraud, larceny, and robbery, whereby the Roman Nimrod and teacher of sin peddles sin and hell to the whole world and sucks and entices away everybody's money as the price of this unspeakable harm."[2]

Yet, October 31, 1517 is still considered the beginning of the Protestant Reformation. Luther's *Theses*—the words that sparked the movement to recover the purity of the apostolic message lost in medieval Christianity—started a revolution within the church that could never be undone. "Out of love and concern for the truth, and with the object of eliciting it," he began his document, troubled over the abuses inherent in the church into which he was born and raised and to which he had devoted his life. Although before he even considered the possibility of disputing the established hierarchy, he first endured a profound spiritual thunderstorm that took years before it finally abated. Luther spent decades in torment and fear before he could proclaim with the apostle Paul: "We have peace with God" (Rom 5:1).

Martin Luther, a promising twenty-two-year-old university student, was returning to his home from the university when, on a sultry July day in 1505, the sky suddenly became overcast; there was a shower, and then a tumultuous storm. Young Luther was knocked to the ground by a burst of lightning and, fearing for his life, cried out in terror, "St. Anne, help me! I will become a monk." He was raised in a superstitious family where he'd been taught that God's wrath pours down indiscriminately upon unsuspecting creatures. Luther feared on that fateful day he might be God's next victim.

2. Ibid.

The storm eventually passed; the student survived the encounter with nature, but remained true to his promise to become a monk. For it was in that moment, in that treacherous storm, that the single flash awakened Luther to the realization there was a vengeful God who poured out his wrath upon wicked creatures. So, like most other people living in the Middle Ages, this man knew what he ought to do, just as the church had taught—he must appease God's wrath. To accomplish this, he would keep his vow to St. Anne and join a strict monastery, the reformed congregation of the Augustinians. This decision, however, displeased his family. Luther's father wanted him to pursue a different occupation, preferably law, so that in his old age, Luther would be in a financial situation in which he could take care of his parents.

The day Luther arrived at the monastery gates, he resolved to be the best monk possible. With an unparalleled intensity, he went beyond the normal limits requested of him. Luther wore himself out with self-flagellation, fasting, and prayers. The dreadful thought that he might go to the confessional and forget to mention a sin haunted him. He exhausted his superiors with his endless confessions and, on one occasion, spent nearly six hours in the confessional asking forgiveness. On one occasion, his advisor finally told him, "If you expect Christ to forgive you, come in with something to forgive—patricide, blasphemy, adultery—instead of these peccadilloes."[3] He later recalled that if ever a monk was able to merit heaven through monkery, it would have been he. Yet, despite his best offerings, and the promises of the church, his herculean efforts were not enough to bring peace to his tormented soul. Something about his natural condition terrified him; he felt he had no protection from God's wrath.

Perhaps no other event crystallizes the depth of Luther's fear as when he said his first mass. Uttering the Latin formula and holding the consecrated wine, he was, as he later recalled, "utterly stupefied and terror-stricken" at the thought of lifting his eyes and hands before an Almighty God. What if he said the wrong words or dropped the blood of Christ? Would God, in all his manifest and righteous anger, strike him dead, he wondered? The possibility of an egregious mistake was too much for him to overcome. Luther, paralyzed with fright, was unable to continue the mass, much to the chagrin of his family and friends who had made the long journey to see him.

---

3. Ibid., 41.

Soon thereafter, his friend and superior, Johann Staupitz, was able to secure for him a teaching position as a professor of Bible in Wittenberg. Staupitz thought a change of scenery would do well for Luther's mind and soul. Though reluctant at first, Luther accepted the position and began teaching through the Bible.

Somewhere along the way while studying through Romans, Luther came to see God in an entirely new light. The guilt and fear that consumed his every waking thought was ameliorated by the uncomplicated phrase: "The righteous shall live by faith" (1:17). It was at this moment that he grasped the justice of God via righteousness by which, through his own grace and mercy, he justifies sinners through the gift of faith. Luther later recalled he felt himself free of the guilt and sin that had plagued him for so long. The entirety of Scripture took on a new, vibrant meaning. Formerly, he heard about the justice of God and was filled with hate; now the phrase took on a completely and inexpressible new reflection—the reflection of profound love. The gate to paradise was opened for Luther, but only after he stopped trying to earn his way into heaven.

Still a professor and preacher at the church in Wittenberg, he began to teach his congregants of his newfound convictions. It was also at about this time that the monk, Tetzel, a representative of Pope Leo X, was selling indulgences in the nearby town in order to raise money to finance the construction of St. Peter's Cathedral in Rome.

Luther's keen awareness of Tetzel and his misrepresentation of the church's doctrine raised great indignation against the entire episode. He ruminated over the matter and drafted his *95 Theses*, as mentioned previously. It should be recognized that his reflections upon the matter went beyond the mere questioning of the efficacy of indulgences. In fact, he went further in his condemnation and exposed the exploitation that was at the heart of the issue. If it is true, Luther reasoned, that the pope has the authority to free souls from purgatory, he ought to use that divine power and free every last one without financial compensation. Moreover, the pope ought to give money liberally to the poor and needy, even if it meant selling the Basilica of St. Peter. So with these conflicting feelings and emotions, Luther nailed his *Theses* to the church door and waited for a response.

What was intended to be a scholarly discussion turned into a firestorm of controversy after someone removed the *Theses* and took them to the printing press for mass production. Within weeks, copies were made and distributed across Germany.

When word of the episode reached the Vatican, the pope's response was to ask someone in the Augustinian order to deal with the matter since Luther was one of its members. Luther was called to the next meeting, almost expecting to be condemned as a heretic and burned at the stake. Yet, what he discovered was that many of his fellow friars were supportive of his position and enthusiastic about his overt protests. Others, though, viewed the episode as a rivalry between Dominicans and Augustinians, and consequently refused to abandon the cause for the latter. In the final analysis, Luther was strengthened in personal resolve and public sentiment and was encouraged by his fellow colleagues.

The Roman magisterium, by contrast, was not pleased with Luther's seeming obstinacy. A diet was convened in order to settle the matter of the troublesome preacher, and it was at Worms in 1521 where, recalling the tenacity of Huss, he stood firmly when asked to recant by responding, "My conscience is a prisoner of God's Word. I cannot and will not recant, for to disobey one's conscience is neither just nor safe. God help me. Amen."[4]

The dividing line had been drawn, and Luther was ready for the ensuing epoch-making battle. Pope Leo X responded this time more assertively by issuing a papal bull in which he declared Luther to be a wild bull that had barged into the Lord's vineyard. The document ordered his books to be burned and provided the monk sixty days to repent before he was to be excommunicated, that is, cut off with the eternal anathema.

Officially branded a heretic and schismatic, excommunicated, banished, and condemned by religious and secular authorities, Luther was kidnapped by friends on a return journey home. Unaware of the plot to save his life, Luther was taken and protected in a castle by friend and admirer, Duke Frederick of Saxony. While resting in the confines of safety, he poured his energy into studying the Word of God, reflecting upon the dogmas of the Roman Catholic Church, writing copiously, and translating the New Testament into the German tongue.

After a year in seclusion, Luther returned to Wittenberg where he confronted the crisis that was brewing. Over the course of his one-year absence, his ideas had spread like wildfire across Europe, his views gushing forth like water bursting from a dam. The fire had been lighted, and no one was going to put it out.

4. Quoted in Gonzalez, *The Story of Christianity: The Reformation to the Present Day*, 28.

Among the many changes Luther initiated in the Reformation was to quash the antiquated and unbiblical notion that priests were to remain celibate. After all, some of the apostles were married, and Paul makes it abundantly clear that marriage is good and necessary and an institution ordained by God. Luther, therefore, married a former nun, Kathryn von Bora. Together they had six children and raised four other orphans, which gave him a fresh perspective on life. Somewhere along the line of his journey into fatherhood, he concluded "marriage is a far better school for character than any monastery."[5]

THE RADICAL REFORMATION

Luther was convinced that, over the course of centuries, the church had been perverted and had ceased being a New Testament church. Ulrich Zwingli (1484–1531), a Swiss contemporary and fellow Reformer, agreed on this point but went further, teaching that only measures which have clear scriptural basis should be believed and practiced. But then there were some who pointed out that Zwingli was not consistent with his teachings. These individuals agreed with his initial premise but sought to carry his beliefs to their logical end.

Critical of the Roman Catholic Church—but also disenchanted with certain aspects of Luther's and Zwingli's teachings—these people argued the New Testament church knew of no compromise with the state, and co-mingling with civil rulers resulted only as a consequence of Constantine's meddling in church affairs. By bringing the two entities together, these radicals argued, the church betrayed the simplicity of the apostolic ideal. If Christians were truly to be faithful to the principles championed by Luther and others, they must be consistent and go much further than the Reformers. The church cannot be confused with the state, and merely being born into the church—in contrast with the state—does not automatically guarantee one is a member of the same without a personal, conscious decision. For this reason, infant baptism must be rejected, since it assumes all those who are baptized as infants become Christians. After all, they reasoned, a personal choice for Christ stands at the heart of the Christian faith.

Most of these radicals who sought greater reform were also pacifists, interpreting the Sermon on the Mount as prescriptive of the

---

5. Glimpses, "Martin Luther; Monumental Reformer," lines 104–5.

Christian life. Those who opposed such beliefs and took up arms in defense of themselves, they contended, lack genuine faith in a sovereign God. This particular belief was not well received in Luther's Germany or in Zwingli's Switzerland. The former were in constant fear of Turkish invaders, while the latter were always in danger of being annihilated by Roman Catholic armies.

These were some of the central beliefs of the radicals. These core teachings, in some varying form or another, circulated throughout Europe and influenced many in differing ways, including nations that were decidedly Roman Catholic. But it was in Zurich that significant attention was given. There, a group of individuals, who called themselves "brethren," urged Zwingli to take a decisive stance against the Roman Church, to exceed Luther in his preaching, and to form a new congregation. When Zwingli refused to capitulate to the mounting pressure, the group of brethren proceeded in reform without his approbation or consent. As it was, George Blaurock, a former priest, asked another brethren, Conrad Grebel, to baptize him. So on January 21, 1525, Blaurock was baptized in Zurich, and he, then, in turn, administered the rite to others.

News of the event travelled quickly throughout the countryside, and opponents began using the pejorative term, "Anabaptist," or "rebaptizer". To the radicals, however, they were not being re-baptized since the first baptism during infancy, so far as they could tell, was invalid. Be that as it may, history knows this group of radicals as Anabaptists—a group who, ironically, was viscerally opposed by both Roman Catholics and Protestants (Reformed and Lutheran) alike.

The new movement drew condemnation from advocates on both sides of the theological issue. Catholics persecuted the Anabaptist for heresy and schism; Protestants took a general distrust of the radicals, not so much for questioning the rite of baptism (though some inevitably did), but rather for denying the integral role of the state as it relates to the church. Most Protestants feared Anabaptists would threaten the fabric of the reform movement and upset the social order amidst the already precarious political climate and upheavals of the sixteenth century.

One practical problem with drawing a contrast between the two was that, even if not originally intended, the reality was that Lutheranism in Germany was supported by the princes, and similarly, in Zurich, the Council of Government held the final word in ecclesiastical matters. By contrast, the radical reformers wanted to eradicate all forms of civil jurisdiction and influence within the church. Instead, they advocated an egalitarian form of rule within the church, which included an unprecedented structure of having men and women, rich and poor, educated and illiterate all possess equal rights.

To outsiders, the Anabaptist movement appeared to be seditious. Beginning in 1525 in the Roman Catholic areas of Switzerland, the authorities condemned its followers to death. Quickly following suit, the civil authorities in Protestant lands even ordered Anabaptists to be put to death on the basis of ancient laws, although some rulers refused. Since the Anabaptists were accused of heresy and sedition, both ecclesiastical and civil authorities demanded vindication over those who would be charged with the crimes.

Draconian policies ensued and countless Anabaptists were martyred for their "radical" beliefs. In total, estimates have put the number of deaths at more than all the early Christian martyrs up to the time of Constantine. While the manner of victimization varied from location to location, most persecution ended with the same result—death. With brutal irony, radical reformers who were captured were oftentimes drowned, drawn and quartered, beheaded, beaten, burned, or pressed to death with heavy stones.

As one might expect when people are unjustly put to death for a cause, legends sprouted, stories romanticized its martyrs, and acts of heroism swept across the continent. In the end, as the persecution reached its climax—just as in the first few centuries after the life of Christ—the "radical" Christian movement continued to germinate throughout Europe, influencing later groups such as the Baptists, Mennonites, Puritan Separatists, Quakers, Amish, Hutterites, and many others.

JOHN CALVIN, THE GREAT SYSTEMATIZER

Ruminating upon the created world around him, Calvin observed: "There is not one blade of grass, there is no color in this world that is not intended to make us rejoice." Those words, demonstrating a profound appreciation for happiness and joy, were penned by a man who many claimed produced a joyless Christianity. His very name evokes passion and deep-seated feelings, as he is most remembered as the Reformer who stressed predestination and election, an idea that stands at open variance with many evangelicals today. But those who have taken the time to study Calvin and his doctrines at any length are not surprised to discover a deep love and appreciation for the father of Presbyterianism. Nor are they surprised that he would utter such a sentiment about joy in the world from the brilliant colors of nature.

Born a generation later than Luther in Noyon, France in 1509, John Calvin was intended to be a priest. At the University of Paris, he studied Latin and theology, but later entered the field of law at Orleans. Around the year 1533, after finishing his studies—and a year after publishing a commentary on the Roman philosopher Seneca's *De Clementia*—Calvin recalled that he was struck with a "sudden conversion".

After coming into contact with the writings of Luther, his heart was subdued, and he gained the sudden realization that the sacramental system of grace offered by the Roman Church was insufficient. He broke with Catholicism and openly spoke out against her teachings. By 1536, he published his first edition of the monumental handbook of Protestant theology, *The Institutes of the Christian Religion*, which to this day stands par excellence as a summary of Christian beliefs. By the age of twenty-seven, he had already gained a reputation for being a clear articulator of the Reformation faith.

When conditions became unsafe in Paris, he retreated from the city and was headed to Strasbourg in the northeast part of the country. As it happened, along the way, by providence, he passed through the city of Geneva in Switzerland, intending on only staying the night. When the Reformer of Geneva, Guillaume Farel, discovered Calvin was in the city, he pressed him to stay and to help the reform movement.

Reluctant at first, Farel finally convinced Calvin that he needed to stay in the city and administer reform or face the displeasure of God. Calvin finally capitulated, staying in the city which served as his home until he died in 1564—the only exception being a three-year period during which he was exiled for his strict conduct, only to be invited back to a position of leadership.

In Geneva, his workload was staggering by any comparison and his accomplishments, remarkable. Calvin pastored at the St. Pierre church where he preached daily. He wrote voluminously, producing commentaries on the Old and New Testaments, writing dozens of pamphlets on Christian doctrine and devotions, penning copious amounts of theological correspondence, and training missionaries to send to all parts of the world. He was able to manage all of this while constantly battling various physical ailments, including chronic sickness and migraine headaches.

The Reformer rarely slept more than four hours a day, which probably contributed to his rapidly deteriorating health.

Calvin's idea was to transform Geneva into the kingdom of God on earth. He had very explicit ideas of what the model city should be like and, in order to accomplish his vision, he would have to implement, from a modern perspective, draconian measures. He was constantly at odds with the Libertines in the city, those who were without religious compunction and who lacked morals before his arrival. So when Calvin attempted moral reform in the community, many balked at his efforts. Yet, before long, his influence touched nearly every aspect of city life. And just like the Catholic Church did with her denizens who fell out of line, Calvin urged excommunication of church members whose personal living standards were at odds with the Christian way of life. More than this, every citizen of the city was required to subscribe to the city council's confession, whether they agreed with it or not.

Dissenters eventually complied with the city's policy, and because of the moral reforms enacted, Geneva became a refuge for Protestants across all of Europe seeking protection. It also functioned as the closest city possible to a Reformed utopia. Even the Scot Reformer, John Knox, referred to the city as the most perfect institution since the time of the apostles. Calvin's acute mind and legal training enabled him to bring civil structure to the city, while his theological understanding permitted a renewed appreciation, vigor, and understanding of the Reformation faith, most notably due to his *Institutes*.

It was Calvin's indefatigable work in the production of his massive work that earned him the reputation as the great systematizer of the Protestant Reformation. Though Luther and others wrote voluminously about such doctrines as God's sovereignty, fallen man, predestination, and election, no one ever stated so clearly and succinctly these doctrines and laid them out in a systematic manner. Calvin, seemingly without equal, was able to bring together the key elements of the faith. From the knowledge of God to the form of civil government, Calvin expressly laid out the fundamental beliefs that encapsulated the Reformation ideals.

Amazingly enough, however, it is the doctrines propounded in his book three that has garnered the most attention—and not to mention the most animosity. While exploring the role of the Holy Spirit in the salvific process, Calvin taught that regeneration is only possible through the Spirit's efficacious enablement in sinners. For Calvin, salvation was only possible through an act of divine grace. But then he went even further. Continuing, he concluded that before the foundations of the earth were laid, God chose some men and angels to eternal life through Jesus Christ to the praise of his grace, while others are left willingly and freely to revel in their own sin, leading to their just condemnation and destruction.

Yet, ironically, though much controversy has surrounded Calvin concerning his beliefs, his ideas were not peculiar. Augustine, believing he had scriptural grounds from which to teach his views of election and predestination, unequivocally taught the same concepts centuries earlier. Luther also firmly embraced these teachings, as did the overwhelming majority of Reformers.

It was Calvin, nonetheless, who stated the doctrines with such forcefulness and clarity that they have since been identified with his name, especially given that the Synod of Dort (1618–1619) appealed to his writings when rejecting the teachings of Jacob Arminius. So for Calvin and the Reformers, the idea that God ordained a specific people to salvation is clearly taught in Scripture and is integral to the whole of the Christian faith.

Sovereignty, for Calvin—followed closely by the fallen nature of mankind—was the starting point from which everything else logically follows. Growing up in the Roman tradition, Calvin came to despise sacramentalism and the view that salvation degenerated into a works-based human endeavor. The constant theme of his theology, then, was the same as the other Reformers: God "does according to his will among the host of the heaven and among the inhabitants of the earth" (Dan 4:35). God must first work a miracle of grace in the heart of unbelievers in order to free the enslaved nature. Just as the prophet exclaimed, the Lord will take away the heart of stone and replace it with a heart of flesh (Ezek 36:26). Salvation, from beginning to end, is of the Lord.

Since only God knows who belongs among the elect, a moral life demonstrates to the world that a person is (probably) one of the elect. Calvin was able to master the flesh and was intensely devoted to righteous living, and he inculcated in others the need, as Paul said, to work out one's salvation, not to be justified before God but to prove regeneration has occurred. This major emphasis on Christian living acted to transform a wicked and sinful world through evangelism and personal conduct—one of the principle characteristics of Calvinism.

Calvin's theology, without question, was imported throughout Europe and the New World more so than any other stripe of Protestantism. So influential was his theology that his spiritual descendants comprise the World Alliance of Reformed churches based in Geneva. In total, this alliance consists of some 178 denominations and more than 50 million followers in more than 80 countries around the world.

THE ROMAN CATHOLIC RESPONSE TO THE PROTESTANT REFORMATION

On more than one occasion, Luther and others appealed to the pope to convoke an ecumenical council to discuss many of the festering issues. However, the Roman See devoted the early years following Luther's *Theses* in attempting to suppress the new teachings instead of seeking reform. Popes opposed such gatherings, as they feared an assembly could be used—as it had in the recent past—to assert authority and control over the pope. For this reason, it would not be until the break between Roman Catholics and Protestants was completed that serious consideration was given to any notion of calling a council for the purpose of reform.

As it was, the Roman Catholic Church selected the northern Italian city of Trent to convene the council in December of 1545. The first session of the "ecumenical" council seated thirty-one participants, with the number increasing to just over two-hundred in attendance at the final session. Starting early the following year, the Council of Trent set forth irreversible Roman dogmas, which marked the theological birth of the modern Roman Catholic Church.

Until the time of Trent, the majority of the previous councils dealt with only a few concerns or a particular heretical doctrine that posed a threat to the church. Protestantism, however, changed the scope, and because of the magnitude of issues that needed resolution or answers, this council felt the necessity of meticulously going through the distinctives of the theology of the Protestant Reformers and issuing decrees. More than this, though, the council took additional measures to address the life and worship of the church.

From 1545 until the last session in 1563—with much of the council spent in suspension for a number of political and theological maneuverings—Trent issued an extensive list of condemnations, measures, and ecclesiastical reforms. The practice of pluralism (holding more than one church office) was forbidden, relics and indulgences were regulated, and seminaries were to be opened for the express purpose of propagating Roman theological training, with the study of Thomas Aquinas at the fore. Trent made his theology the dominant theology of the church.

In contrast to Protestantism, the council officially and dogmatically adopted the apocryphal books of the Old Testament, declared the Latin Vulgate to be the authoritative translation of the Bible, acknowledged both tradition and Scripture as equally authoritative, established the number of the sacraments at seven, affirmed the mass as a true and propitiatory sacrifice, and (most poignantly) declared the foundation of a believer's justification to include God's grace and the believer's own good works. Regarding the latter, canon IX of session VI states: "If any one saith that by faith alone the impious is justified, in such wise as to mean, that nothing else is required to cooperate in order to obtain the grace of justification . . . let him be anathema." Clearly, then, the dividing line had been drawn, and the schism would persist.

Though diminutive in number, and despite fierce resistance from civil rulers in certain parts of Europe, the Council of Trent marked the beginning of modern Roman Catholic theology. The chance of healing the rupture was, henceforth, impossible because Protestants would not accept tradition as being "God-breathed" and equally authoritative as Scripture; nor would they deny the concept that salvation is by grace alone through faith alone on account of Christ alone.

With supreme power given to the bishop of Rome, Trent marked the triumph of papal absolutism and set the Roman Church on an irreversible course from which she could never turn back. She placed herself in a position whereby she could never be corrected since she was, as she claimed, the authoritative voice in regard to the meaning of both Scripture and tradition. Rome's reforms did not go far enough, and so far as Protestants were concerned, they were heading in the wrong direction.

WHAT DOES IT MEAN TO BE A PROTESTANT?

In his review of the co-authored book by Mark Noll and Carolyn Nystrom, *Is the Reformation Over? An Evangelical Assessment of Contemporary Roman Catholicism*, Carl Trueman expressed this sentiment regarding what it means to be a Protestant:

> "... we need good, solid reasons for not being Catholic; not being Catholic should, in other words, be a positive act of will and commitment, something we need to get out of bed determined to do each and every day. It would seem, however, that if Noll and Nystrom are correct, many who call themselves evangelical really lack any good reason for such an act of will; and the obvious conclusion, therefore, should be that they do the decent thing and rejoin the Roman Catholic Church."[6]

Trueman goes on to say that, for him, his views of justification by faith and ecclesiology preclude him from being a Roman Catholic. Yet, for many professing evangelicals, their reason for being non-Catholic is not so clear and, in reality, seems a bit anemic and unconvincing.

If the Protestant is unable to rise in the morning and muster compelling and decisive reasons why he is not a Catholic, then he is merely perpetuating an act of schism, which is without biblical and rational warrant. If, however, non-Catholics can rise up in the morning and determinedly walk down the pathway which believers such as Calvin, Luther, Zwingli and others prepared long before their births, then they rightly understand what it means to be a Protestant.

Understanding what the Reformation was all about is to recognize what it means to be Protestant and evangelical. Arguably the foremost general principle of the Protestant Reformation included the idea of scriptural religion. That is, the Church of Rome had dethroned the Bible from its rightful supremacy and had essentially withheld the vernacular Scriptures from the people.[7] Filling this void, then, was the so-called

---

6. Beckwith, *Return to Rome: Confessions of an Evangelical Catholic*, 83.

7. Session XXV of the Council of Trent, on 'Rules Concerning Prohibited Books Drawn Up by The Fathers': "Since it is clear from experience that if the Sacred Books are permitted everywhere and without discrimination in the vernacular, there will by reason of the boldness of men arise there from more harm than good, the matter is in this respect left to the judgment of the bishop or inquisitor, who may with the advice of the pastor or confessor permit the reading of the Sacred Books translated into the vernacular by Catholic authors to those who they know will derive from such reading no harm but rather an increase of faith and piety, which permission they must have in writing. Those, however, who presume to read or possess them without such permission may not receive absolution from their sins till they have handed over to the ordinary. Book dealers who sell or in any way supply Bibles written in the vernacular to anyone who has not this permission, shall lose the price of the books, which is to be applied by the bishop to pious purposes, and in keeping with the nature of the crime they shall be subject to other penalties which are left to the judgment of the same bishop. Regulars who have not the permission of their superiors may not read or purchase them." As

infallible pope and teaching magisterium, who, when exercising apostolic authority, could not error in matters of faith and morals. Today, this sentiment is just as important to the fabric of the institution and is held as doggedly by Roman Catholic faithful as when it was first introduced.

Indeed, Rome claims she alone possesses infallibility, and as such, is the ultimate judge of what is and is not Scripture; what is and is not the meaning of Scripture; what is and is not tradition; and what is and is not the meaning of tradition. Given, then, the reality that neither Scripture nor tradition can ever correct Rome—since she alone, *sola Romanus*, defines the extent and meaning of both—she necessarily is the *ultimate* authority and sole source of all truth.

The Reformers corrected this manifest usurping of authority by reinstituting the rightful place of the Word of God in the church and subordinating all doctrines to Scripture. Moreover, the Reformers believed every person has a right and a duty to read the Bible in his own language. The Roman Church had, slowly and over the course of several centuries, introduced concepts that were foreign to Scripture. Transubstantiation, image-worship, papal pretensions, the Assumption of Mary, purgatory, and many other dogmas were incorporated into Roman Church ritual, all of which resulted from abandoning the practice of *sola Scriptura*.

Recognizing the rightful need for revelation before binding any doctrine on the conscience of believers, the Reformers demanded absolute fidelity to God's Word. Anything not directly supported by Scripture was to be jettisoned, or at least held in abeyance. Because the Bible is immutable and because it is literally "breathed-out by God," Scripture alone is the supreme authoritative voice in the church.

As a consequence of abandoning the ultimate authority of the Bible, the Roman Catholic Church practically discouraged personal access of the human soul to God. Standing between the creature and Creator, the pope, councils, and bishops interposed their authority and spiritual jurisdiction over all professing believers. Between the soul stained with iniquities and divine remission of sins the priest intervened with purported absolution, the ability to forgive sins. The meritorious works of Jesus, Mary, and the saints were made to interject on behalf of sinners, with salvation being mediated through the sacramental system of Rome. Indeed, the sacraments of the church were said to be "channels of grace," the means by which God applied the grace of salvation to the lost.

---

cited in Schroeder, *Canons and Decrees of the Council of Trent*, 274–75.

In response, the Reformers rejected all such barriers to personal salvation and declared the right of private judgment, proclaimed the priesthood of every believer, and emphasized personal responsibility of each individual before God, yet without devaluing the role of the church or her authority. The Reformers opposed the concept that grace makes humans inherently pleasing toward God and, when placed in a state of grace, we perform good works that serve as the basis for salvation. Rather, they emphasized that salvation is wholly of God.

The groundwork of human salvation is found in and through the perfect righteousness of Christ. When God looks at believers, he sees them as if they are cloaked in Christ's righteousness, and as such, declares them to be not guilty. Luther declared the true and decisive factor in determining if a local organization is truly a church can be boiled down to this one issue—justification. It is the article, he argued, by which the church stands or falls.

So with this in mind, we return to our question: "What does it mean, historically speaking, to be a Protestant?" Simply stated, non-Catholics accept the Bible as the ultimate authority for the church, which covers all things necessary concerning God's glory, mankind's salvation, and faith and life. Not only this, but that Scripture is perspicacious as well. From the opening sentence of the Bible, "In the beginning, God," God's people find the simplicity of Holy Scripture revealing the origins of the universe and continuing onward from there. God's Word gives light to those who earnestly seek the truth, enough so that even the simplest minds can know what God requires of them to gain entrance into heaven.

When Paul wrote to the Galatians that "if anyone is preaching to you a gospel contrary to the one you received, let him be accursed" (Gal 1:8–9), he was indicating an important truism. The very fact that Paul commanded his audience to judge the message, regardless of who spoke it (which included himself as well as the words of any of the apostles), goes to show God commands individuals to use human faculties. The Galatians were not to submit their minds to the unsubstantiated claims of mere men, even those holding position and stature within the visible church. Instead, they were instructed to use their own discernment and reasoning skills to determine if a claim was true by comparing it to God's Word. Moreover, Paul's instruction in this manner presupposes or assumes mankind's ability to exercise private judgment soundly and to reach a knowable conclusion apart from any suggested infallible interpreter.

More than this, being a Protestant means accepting the reformational view of God, of humanity, of sin, and of salvation. If we truly recognize God's sovereignty and creatorial rights over his creation, then we understand that salvation can have no barriers in the salvific process. The one who approaches the text of Scripture free of external, human traditions will realize that God cannot be contained by mankind in any concept or system of sacraments. That said, neither can salvation be abrogated through the unwillingness of humankind. God is far too great and powerful to be limited by diminutive efforts of humans to earn or to merit Christ's grace, nor can the perfect righteousness of the Lord be appropriated through the intents and purposes of any mortal creature. When God chooses to bestow grace upon his creation, he does so to the expressed pleasure that brings him the most glory and honor.

Throughout the history of the church, God-centered theology has been under attack and oftentimes replaced with human-centered beliefs. Over the years, this has been manifested in many different ways and has taken shape through differing theological paradigms. Yet, the two positions—though recycled in new dress—always boil down to this: monergism versus synergism. In the end, we must ask ourselves if we are willing to embrace the orthodox Protestant view of monergistic salvation so that we might willingly stand in the tradition of our spiritual forefathers and give God all the praise and glory.

In the final analysis, if we do not adhere to the Reformed view of God's sovereignty, the nature of man, predestination and election, and free will, why do we call ourselves Protestant? If we are not willing to take the Reformed gospel as rediscovered in the sixteenth century, then why do we insist on remaining non-Catholics? If the differences between post-Tridentine Rome and current evangelicalism are not significant, why do we insist on perpetuating this schism?

If, however, the Reformers were correct and the differences touch upon the gospel itself, then we must be faithful to the Protestant tradition or, as Trueman rightly pointed out, we must do the decent thing and return home to Rome. Either we proclaim *soli Deo Gloria*, to God alone be the glory for his act in the salvation of sinners, or we adopt the concept of *sola Romanus*, Rome alone. We cannot, on the one hand, deny Rome, and yet embrace her view of salvation. There is no hybrid which can be constructed between the two. We either stand in the tradition of the Reformation or turn our backs on the Reformers and the Bible.

"Choose this day whom you will serve, whether the gods your fathers served in the region beyond the River, or the gods of the Amorites in whose land you dwell. But as for me and my house, we will serve the LORD" (Josh 24:15).

Think About It

1. What was Luther's main problem as a monk?
2. What does Paul mean when he says, "we have peace with God" (Rom 5:1)?
3. What is the basis of our having peace with God?
4. Is there a helper on earth today, guiding believers (the church) into truth?
5. Why are you a Protestant?

8

The Church in North America

(1607–Present)

INITIAL BRITISH ATTEMPTS AT colonizing North America were unsuccessful. Beginning in 1584, Queen Elizabeth granted a royal charter to Sir Walter Raleigh to colonize North America. The land he set out to inhabit would be named in honor of the "Virgin Queen"—Virginia. But, alas, his two expeditions, one in 1585 and the second in 1587, failed to achieve the desired result. Disconcerted with the future prospects of the colony and ill-prepared for surviving off the land, the settlers abandoned the settlement and returned home to England. The second attempt at colonizing North America was even less successful as it ended in complete mystery, with the settlers simply disappearing.

It would not be until 1607 that 105 settlers landed near the mouth of the James River—so named in honor of the new English monarch. This village, called Jamestown, became the first permanent English settlement in America. Among the first settlers to arrive was the Reverend Robert Hunt who accompanied the crew in order to establish the Church of England in the new land. More than this, many English pioneers were hopeful the propagation of Protestantism throughout the New World would facilitate the abatement of Spanish expansion to the north and thus, the spread of Roman Catholicism as well.

Despite the earnest desire of Hunt to see the Jamestown settlement flourish with settlers who were committed to Christian living, the lives of the early colonists lacked cohesion and godly devotion. The settlement was nearly wrecked because of chaos, fighting, pride, arrogance, and greed. The earliest pioneers had little room for God in their personal lives and clearly had no inclination of evangelizing the native peoples.

All of this manifest selfishness culminated in disease, famine, and Indian attacks, which decimated Jamestown. Nine out of every ten colonists perished. As the town was resupplied from England, the problems only seemed exacerbated, and the death toll continued to mount.

Nevertheless, there were still many in England who continued to think of America in terms of God's purposeful plan for a new beginning with religious freedom. It was in 1609 that William Symonds preached a sermon to landowners living in England, comparing Virginia to the biblical Promised Land flowing with milk and honey. Just as Caleb and Joshua persisted in encouraging Moses to enter Canaan, Symonds urged his countrymen to take their possessions and head for Jamestown, the land gifted with bountiful blessings.

And so it was that in 1609, a third ship, the Sea Venture, replete with provisions and settlers set sail for Virginia. The ship, while just off the coast of Bermuda, encountered a hurricane with tumultuous seas and deadly winds and shipwrecked, but all passengers onboard were able to make it to shore safely. Not yet discouraged at facing their daunting prospects, the people were able to reconstruct a ship from the wreckage, which they then sailed to Virginia, reaching its shores a year later.

When the people arrived, they were horrified at the near ruins of the fort. Though the group had seemingly lost hope and were ready to return to England, Lord de La Warr (whose name was given to the state, Delaware) providentially arrived from England with much needed supplies and more colonists. To the colonists, de La Warr's arrival was seen as an act of divine intervention. God knew their needs and provided for them. The new colonial governor, de La Warr, also recognized God's hand in the affair and organized a worship service, which helped inspire a renewed emphasis on the biblical role of hard work and industry among the people.

Ironically, one of the passengers who survived the hurricane and shipwreck was a man named John Rolfe. A hardworking man of principle, he was a devout Calvinist who sought to advance the glory of God and propagate the gospel. Jamestown, he believed, was divinely ordained. As it turned out, while in Virginia, he met the daughter of the Indian chief, Powhatan, but was unsure if it was God's will for him to marry a heathen. He resolved to minister to the young woman, to plant the seed of the gospel, and to pray for her conversion. God answered his prayers. After Pocahontas' conversion to Christianity, she took the Christian name of Rebecca, and she became John Rolfe's wife.

Rolfe, however, was not the only devout Christian in the Virginia settlement. Though not originally established as a religious outpost, many of the colonists were, however, of Calvinistic Puritan heritage. Because of this religious influence, the colony was ruled by Puritan principles. Practically speaking, what this meant was that a man who did not work did not eat. Also, attendance at worship service was required twice a day, as was a fastidious adherence to the Lord's Day. Profane speech and immodest dress was also prohibited. Yet, such rigid rules were quickly abandoned after King James I—who detested Puritanism for its attempt to reform the Church of England—placed the colony directly under his rule after the settlers engaged in a war with American Indians. In so doing, James reversed some of the Puritan rules and enacted policies that stood at open variance with many of the Protestant ideals, and as such, Puritanism in the early colony waned.

Further north, most notably in the colonies of Massachusetts and Connecticut, Puritanism made its greatest impact, while the middle and southern colonies were influenced the greatest by a mixture of Quakers, Catholics, Lutherans, Anglicans, Methodists, and Baptists.

PURITAN INFLUENCE IN NEW ENGLAND

It was in the northern colonies that Puritanism made the most monumental advances. In the region that became known as New England, the Puritan spirit and ideal shaped the new land, becoming the most dynamic strength in the American colonies. Originally from England, the Puritans were individuals who were, in many instances, of political influence or financial means. These devoted Christians attempted to reform the Church of England, but King Charles—acting much like the bishop of Rome during the sixteenth century—refused to tolerate their attempts at bringing change to the church.

The name "Puritan" was originally designed to be a pejorative term. It was first used during the reign of Queen Elizabeth in attempting to ridicule Christians who wanted to purify the Church of England regarding doctrine, practice, liturgy, and ceremony not found in Scripture. Since the Bible was the sole authority in all matters of faith and practice, they believed it should also be applied to every facet of church life as well.

Because they held publicly to these beliefs, opposition against these Puritans increased and persecution escalated. There was no hope, many thought, except to start life anew in America. Indeed, the Puritans sought to construct an entire society whose government and church were based solely on the Bible. New England would be a shining city upon a hill, exposing the darkness and corruption that was inherent in English society and the established church.

The moment of opportunity came for the Puritans when King Charles granted a charter to the Massachusetts Bay Company but without specifying that its officers and governor had to remain in England. Taking full advantage of this seeming loophole, the Puritan stockholders agreed to move their company to New England where they would attempt to establish a new form of government and society whose foundation was the Bible. There, they would create an example for England and the rest of the world to see. A city dedicated to retaining Christian ideals would be glorifying to God. It was to be the "new Jerusalem".

The Puritan ideal of strong individual faith and conviction did not abrogate their views on family and community. Indeed, many came to America, not as individual families separate from their brothers and sisters in the church, but as entire congregations seeking to start anew in America. Oftentimes led by their ministers, many Englishmen and women left their relatives and the security of their employment to organize a new settlement in an unknown and hostile land. But, once there, they organized into communities with meeting places or churches in the town center. Since God was the central focus of their lives, it was only fitting that each church should be centered in the middle of each town, pointing them toward their Maker and reminding them of their purpose in life.

With an indefatigable work ethic introduced in the Puritan colonies from their Calvinistic convictions, Sundays were devoted fully to resting from the week's labor and also to worshipping the Lord joyfully. Psalms and other Scripture were sung (the first printed book in America was the *Bay Psalm Book*), time was given to prayer, but the central focus of the worship service was the sermon, with a strong emphasis on doctrine and the intellectual life.

The family—the first divine institution—was foundational in Puritan society. Reflecting a picture of Christ and the church, the family was organized and functioned on a minor scale like a church. Mornings and evenings were consumed with family readings, singing, prayer, and devotion. After this time of worship, children were instructed to read, to write, and to be obedient to those in authority so that they would become a source to worship God on their own, bringing glory to Christ.

Within five years of founding the Massachusetts colony, schools were established for children, wherein every one could learn to read the Bible. A few years later, in 1636, the colony established Harvard College in order to train young men for the ministry. The original charter to America's oldest secondary educational institution was committed to Christian ideals and instructing its students to know God and Jesus Christ, the only true foundation for knowledge.

What made Massachusetts so successful was the tenacious belief that every facet of life should be brought into subjection to Christ. That is, every area of life, no matter how seemingly small or trivial, should be done in order to bring glory to God. In that sense, work was viewed as honorable and pleasing to God. No distinction was made between religious work and secular work. All work, according to Christian principles, should be done with a love for and motivation to bring glory to God. Conversely, refusal to work was seen as a great shame and sin. Diligence and industriousness epitomized the Puritan work ethic, bringing assiduousness to one's calling and serving as the basis for the spirit of capitalism.[1]

The secular and religious foundation the Puritans bequeathed to future generations, and consequently to the nation, is unique in world history. Their contribution, both in matters of theology and society, is unmatched, as they proved to be the one group of men and women who had the most profound influence upon the subsequent development of America. Later generations of pioneers and travelers to other parts of the nation, who tamed the land, were often descendents of the Puritans. The values, principles, ethics, and unwavering devotion to God cannot be overstated, nor can it be denied that their influence in American thought and practice continued for centuries after they had passed away.

THE GREAT AWAKENING

Only a few generations removed from when the Puritans first arrived in America, the fervent faith and vision of establishing the ideal Christian utopia was fading quickly. Apathy set in; the religious zeal had abated. Descendants of the original settlers and other non-religious immigrants were more concerned with their own increasing wealth and style of living than they were of advancing the kingdom of God. Such spiritual

---

1. For a fuller treatment of this thesis see Weber, *The Protestant Ethic and the Spirit of Capitalism*.

indifference, however, was not relegated to Massachusetts. In fact, the same religious sentiment could be found throughout all the American colonies, thanks in part to the growing influence of the Enlightenment and the Age of Rationalism. The people of America were so preoccupied with the temporal that they had lost sight of their founding principles.

During the early years of the 1720s, Presbyterian minister, Gilbert Tennent, was greatly influenced by the preaching of a Dutch Reformed minister named Theodore Frelinghuysen. Frelinghuysen first came to New Jersey during this time period and was shocked at the spiritual condition of the general populace. Disconcerted by the growing apathy and perfunctory manner in which many communicants participated, he preached of the need for real and genuine conversion, an experience that resulted in a life-changing commitment to gospel obedience. Tennent picked up on this theme and argued that part of the problem was that some ministers themselves were never genuinely converted. To expand on his thesis, he published his book, *On the Dangers of an Unconverted Ministry*, which created a firestorm of controversy on the subject but not without results in New Jersey.

About the same time, in the year 1727, Jonathan Edwards moved to Northampton, Massachusetts, where he began ministering with his grandfather. After several years of preaching with average results, his sermons, though not necessarily emotive, produced some surprising results. After preaching against the spiritual deadness of the local church, he preached a series in 1734 that convicted the hearts of the people. By December of that year, Edwards recorded in his journal that the Spirit was producing extraordinary results. Over the course of the next few months, some three-hundred people were converted. Soon, the religious movement swept across the area and reached Connecticut. In one of his voluminous writings, Edwards wrote about evidences of true revival and work of the Spirit. Teaching from 1 John 4 about the true nature of salvation, he said that individuals would be confirmed in the truth of the gospel, and that Jesus was the Savior of his people. True converts, therefore, must avoid sin and chasing after the desires of the world; believers would have a greater love for and devotion to Holy Scripture; and finally, that the love for God and for fellow-humans would be manifestly obvious.

Edwards described these salient points in his works and mass produced them for distribution throughout the colonies and in Britain. His intended goal was reached quite remarkably. Ministers on both sides of the Atlantic prayed fervently for revival, and that is exactly what transpired.

About the same time as Edwards was producing results in New England, Anglican minister, George Whitefield, visited Northampton to preach. It is often said that while Whitefield preached from the pulpit, Edwards wept from the pew. His messages were powerful, and his sermons convicted the soul. He firmly insisted that salvation came only through God's irresistible grace. Also an important aspect of his ministry—as was the case with many theologians of his day—was a deep devotion to philanthropic works.

During one of his journeys to America, Whitefield embarked on a year-long tour through the colonies raising money for an orphanage in Georgia. More than this, and perhaps greater so than any other Christian leader of his day, he raised money for a plethora of charitable works, which included schools, libraries, and almshouses in America and in England. So it is of little surprise that Whitefield gained the respect of such notables as Benjamin Franklin.

Franklin was awed by Whitefield when he preached. In his own autobiography, he recounted the enthusiasm that infected him upon hearing Whitefield speak,

> "I happened soon after to attend one of his sermons, in the course of which I perceived he intended to finish with a collection, and I silently resolved he should get nothing from me. I had in my pocket a handful of copper money, three or four silver dollars, and five pistols in gold. As he proceeded I began to soften, and concluded to give the coppers. Another stroke of his oratory made me ashamed of that, and determined me to give the silver; and he finished so admirably, that I emptied my pocket wholly into the collector's dish, gold and all."[2]

Wherever Whitefield traveled and spoke, he drew large crowds, normally numbering in the thousands. Following the preaching and example set forth by Whitefield, local pastors from a variety of Protestant denominations brought a new passion and zeal to the pulpit. Doctrine was reemphasized and extraordinary responses ensued.

The Great Awakening in America during the late 1730s and early 1740s, as it came to be known, produced tremendous results. Church attendance exploded, the number of churches constructed multiplied

---

2. Isaacson, *Benjamin Franklin: An American Life*, 110.

noticeably, scores of thousands were converted en mass—and all this was manifested in a true and demonstrable piety. Christians from across denominational lines worked together to minister to the lost, including missions to the Indians. With such a renewed emphasis on Christian ministry, colleges such as Princeton, Brown, Rutgers, and Dartmouth were formed to meet the new ministerial shortfall.

The Great Awakening in America not only revived the church in the colonies, reemphasized personal experience and conduct, and placed doctrine as central in worship, but it also reinvigorated American society as well. Thanks to the religious sentiment shared by the people throughout the land, a sense of commonality began to develop in the colonies. Combine this with the growing awareness regarding human rights and the limitations of government, and America was on course to produce monumental achievements.

PROTESTANT LIBERALISM AND THE FUNDAMENTALIST RESPONSE

The nineteenth century posed intense intellectual challenges for the church. Roman Catholics generally rejected such claims outright, and argued from the position of ultimate authority. The Protestant response, however, sought ways to capitulate to the overwhelming influence to embrace a new worldview and to interpret the ancient faith in a radically different light. The reaction to both branches of Western Christianity proved to be radically different.

The industrial revolution, by the start of the nineteenth century, had spread across most of Europe and parts of America. Its deep impact influenced more than just economic measures. For many, the entire society and way of life was altered drastically. Instead of living in lands devoted to raising crops, the masses were headed toward the cities, seeking employment in the industrial regions. The traditional view of having extended family members living under one roof was weakened by the transition to city life. Individualism soon became the norm, and it was a common theme in both literature and philosophy.

Not only this, the industrial revolution promoted the idea of progress. Up to this point, the prevailing sentiment throughout much of history had been that proven ideas and practices were better than new and innovative thinking. Even at the time of the Reformation and Enlightenment—a period in which many ideas were introduced—

people sought to return to the simplicity of antiquity in the arts, religion, and knowledge. Now, by contrast, people seemingly jettisoned the past in light of the future. Modern technology by way of applied science produced wealth and many creaturely comforts that were never before available. All of society, many thought, would eventually come to benefit from the fruit of progress in the realm of science and technology. This thinking was prevalent in the writings and teachings of many intellectuals.

In a sense, then, Charles Darwin's theory of evolution was a manifestation of a larger belief in progress, but applied to the realm of natural science. Not only was humankind progressing, but all of nature as well. Nothing in the universe escaped this truism. Advancement and progress, in whatever field, was always on an upward swing. In Darwin's seminal work entitled, *On the Origin of Species by Means of Natural Selection*, he fosters the idea that progress is not always rapid nor is advancement easy. In fact, both are a harsh reality in which the fittest survive and, in so doing, survival is, at the most basic level, an act of progress, which is a contribution to the entire species.

Carrying the Darwinian position to its logical conclusion, as many did, it was argued that since the universe was trending toward progress, it must also follow that history is the same as well. Thus, it was believed that human beings living in the nineteenth century were intellectually superior to those who had lived before them. Primitive views and beliefs about myriad aspects of life, including religion, were seen as just that— superstitious and naive. Typical nineteenth-century intellectuals would argue that they were operating with increased knowledge and a greater awareness of all facets of life in order to make better, more informed decisions about every aspect of the universe.

More important, still, was the belief that if God revealed himself through the evolutionary process, then religion and the Bible must also be viewed through the same lens. The authority and credibility of the Bible was, therefore, called into question. Infallibility and inerrancy were two terms that were mocked as inferior beliefs from previously unenlightened generations.

Liberals, therefore, welcomed what is referred to as "higher criticism," because their approach to the Bible was "necessary for progress". They were happy to abandon the infallibility of God's Word, and they no longer felt compelled to harmonize the Old and New Testament writings as a whole, especially the troubling passages of the Old.

According to the higher critics, God gave revelation in a similar manner. Starting with the bloodthirsty and warring Israelites, God slowly gave more information as time progressed. The Bible outlines how the Jews slowly garnered a fuller understanding of a righteous God who can only be served in and through a righteous walk of faith. This progressive revelation culminated in the fulfillment of all God's promises through the life and obedience of Jesus Christ.

Liberal theologians refused to embrace many of the orthodox teachings passed down through the centuries—especially highly dubious doctrines concerning the Virgin Birth, miracles, Jesus' eternal preexistence, his sinless life, and so on. Emphasis on doctrine was removed and replaced with emotion and feelings. If tenets of the faith could not be validated with the scientific method or through rational inquiry, they were to be discarded. Miracles and other supernatural phenomena were rejected because of this presuppositional approach to reading the Bible. Science—and not faith—was the key to understanding. That is, even though science would not be able to interpret the Bible, it could still tell us the stories handed down in Scripture are outside of the realm of science and therefore should not be trusted.

Not all theologians and Christians, however, were so willing to embrace this new, radical skepticism. Opposition mounted against the Darwinian approach to Scripture and resulted in the Fundamentalist movement. Generally dated from a series of books published between 1910 and 1915, the movement took on the name from the twelve volume florilegium that contained numerous articles and essays designed to defend the fundamental tenets of the Christian religion. Financed by a wealthy oilman from Southern California named Lyman Stewart, the project produced three million copies of *The Fundamentals* and sent them free of charge to Christian ministers, seminarians, and missionaries around the world.

In total, sixty-four authors were eventually chosen who voiced concerns regarding a host of issues including the lapse of several hallmarks of the faith, namely: the trustworthiness of the Bible, the deity of Christ, the physical resurrection, and salvation by grace alone through faith alone, among other definitional doctrines. Notables such as Benjamin B. Warfield of Princeton Seminary, the evangelist, R. A. Torrey and E. Y. Mullins of Southern Baptist Seminary were among those who published articles in the series.

In addition to these men and their voluminous *The Fundamentals*, the Presbyterian scholar, J. Gresham Machen, was another leading guardian of orthodoxy during the early twentieth century. A professor at Princeton Theological Seminary, Machen and other conservatives were troubled when, at the 1929 General Assembly of the Presbyterian Church, the ecclesiastical body granted authorization for the reorganization of the seminary, thus paving the way for increased dissemination of liberal modernist ideas. They withdrew from Princeton in response to this radical paradigm shift and founded Westminster Theological Seminary in Philadelphia.

Not only was Machen forced to contend with liberalism within the realm of academia, but he also encountered it within the Presbyterian Church of the United States of America. Ordered to sever ties with the Independent Board of Presbyterian Foreign Missions, he refused and was brought before an ecclesiastical court. Machen was charged with rebellion against the authorities and was found guilty. As a consequence of that incident, Machen left his Presbyterian Church and formed the Orthodox Presbyterian Church where, to this day, the church remains unaffected by the pernicious influence of liberal skepticism. First among the beliefs is that God's Word, the Bible, is the authoritative God-breathed Scriptures, the only infallible rule of Christian faith and conduct—the essential starting point for orthodoxy and the Fundamentalist movement.

Standing firmly for each of these tenets used to define Fundamentalism. In recent years, however, the term *Fundamentalist* has come to be used in the pejorative sense and is used synonymously for one who holds dogmatically to a view setting aside cause or without the capacity for seeing the other side being presented. It frequently conjures up negative connotations suggesting anti-socialism and anti-intellectualism. Only later, though, did the label *Fundamentalist* come to mean "anti-".

Originally, Fundamentalism meant a strict adherence to the tenets of the Christian faith, believing in the doctrines that were once delivered to the saints. Although there continues to be growing liberalism within several mainline Protestant denominations, the struggle for orthodoxy shows encouraging signs of a comeback in growing movements such as the Presbyterian Church in America, The Lutheran Church (Missouri Synod), and the Southern Baptist Convention.

Liberalism, however, is by no means dead, but with a resurgence in Calvinistic theology across a number of mainline denominations, it can be defeated. The theology of hope is alive and well in many churches throughout America and across the globe, though it is tempered with the reality that God judges and punishes nations for eradicating him from their lives.

THE ANTIDOTE FOR AMERICA

As we have already seen in previous chapters and in the brief snapshot of some essential moments in North American history, the truth remains the same: When the authority of the Bible is abandoned doctrine is corrupted, and society is negatively affected. Yet, even that very statement is not without its own controversy. To postulate that the Bible is the ultimate standard is to suggest that salvation comes through Christ Jesus alone.

Tolerance is often viewed much more highly than doctrinal accuracy or speaking in truth. We have grown accustomed, even within our own churches, to listen to experiences that are devoid of serious doctrinal content. Indeed, the ecumenical movement has, in so many areas, taught us that we must reduce our beliefs to the lowest common denominator in order to find unity. Even when evangelism is attempted, unbelievers are told to embrace Christ, yet they are seldom told why. Rarely is someone told of the sovereignty of God, the radical condition of fallen humanity, or the sufficiency of grace—all of which cannot be adequately known apart from divine Scripture.

It is arguably for this reason that people are abandoning our churches, Sundays are no longer set apart as sacrosanct, and there is a precipitous decline in those who make a commitment or profession to Christ. Easy-believism has gained traction in churches and in the society at large. People "believe" in Christ but have little understanding of what that actually means or what salvation is all about. For this reason, many are easy prey for unstable and untaught men who seduce them with heretical doctrines. This also accounts, in part, for the growing number of sects, cults, and false religions throughout the world.

Such is the consequence of abandoning the simplicity and perspicuity of Holy Scripture, and it is little wonder why doctrine has been subordinated with emotive experience and rank narcissism. By repudiating the beliefs of those who have lived before us, even in our own culture, we are raising up a generation that sees no inherent contradiction in affirming Christ as Lord on Sunday and living according to the flesh the rest of the week. Scandals are plaguing the church, and, sadly, even some of our religious leaders are caught up in a host of ungodly teachings and practices. For far too many people, an understanding of Christianity and the Bible is a mile wide but only an inch deep.

What can the church do to stop this rapid decline? How do we communicate to others the necessity for doctrinal purity and an understanding that the differences are real and that they do actually matter? How are we to overcome this fascination with "unity" at the expense of moral and doctrinal integrity?

The answer, I submit, is God's Word. Understanding the distinctives of the Christian faith as revealed in Scripture is the primary way by which believers garner a pure understanding and appreciation for doctrine. It has become increasingly obvious that one of the primary signs of genuine conversion is found in a person's obedience to, respect of, and love for the Bible. True Christians long to possess the Word, read it, meditate upon its words, and absorb its contents. Strangely, when completely free access to the Bible is available, there appears to be an inverse relationship in which we take it for granted, and as such, we rarely have a zeal for Scripture as compared to those who live in countries where it is banned or unavailable. It is easy to forget those in previous generations who have died for possessing or translating it into the common tongue.

Second, we must understand the past and learn from history. Many battles have been waged over retaining doctrinal purity, so with an intimate knowledge of essential moments in church history we can face future battles with confidence. Imagine the distorted beliefs we might embrace today if no one in the past stood, like Athanasius, against the world. Athanasius refused to accept Arianism, even though the bishop of Rome and the majority of professing believers had already done so. If he was willing to compromise, then he would not have been able to pass down the ancient truths as he did.

Third, we must understand fundamental rules of logic created by God—namely, the law of non-contradiction. This rule essentially states that something cannot both be and not be in the same way, in the same manner, and at the same time. For Christians, then, Jesus cannot both be the only way to God and not be the only way to find salvation. Nor can Christianity be amalgamated with any number of pagan beliefs or superstitions. The integrity of Christian beliefs must be subjected to one unchanging standard on matters of faith and practice—the God-breathed Scriptures.

Finally, the Word provides an authentic model for Christians to follow in their daily thought and conduct. Doctrine influences the way we act. Just look at the Pharisees who thought they were more righteous and more spiritual because of their beliefs. Yet Jesus held them accountable for what was contained in Scripture. "Have you not read?" Jesus repeatedly asked them. Christ challenged their inconsistency in faith and conduct and corrected them by Scripture alone. The importance of the Bible, consequently, cannot be overstated.

We began with the history of God's Word, so it is only fitting that we end in the same place. If we stray from our ultimate authority, the dire consequences are quite obvious. The Bible was sufficient to bring hope and peace to those who were persecuted; it was ample for Athanasius to rebuke the Arians for denying the deity of Christ; it was adequate for Augustine when he argued from Scripture alone concerning the sovereignty of God, the fallen nature of man, and grace in salvation; it was more than enough to censure hierarchy in the established church for preying on the ignorance of the denizens of Europe; it was satisfactory for all who fought and died for the hope of eternal glory; and it was sufficient to see with clarity the abuses which crept into the church after the Bible was forsaken.

When Hilkiah, the Hebrew priest during the reign of King Josiah, rediscovered the Book of the Law, he was spurred to a greater love for God and understood the truth as revealed through Scripture. Real and lasting unity, therefore, is assured only to those who submit to the authority of God's unchanging Word.

We could proceed on indefinitely with the study of this great and profound theme of the written revelation, for we are far from reaching its limit or exhausting its truths. Be that as it may, it is now time that each one takes that step that goes on from theory to daily practice. The great Sovereign of the universe, the great I AM, the King of kings, and Lord of lords longs to reveal his will to us. Our responsibility, therefore, is to drink it up reverently, and meditate upon each inspired word. Then we are commanded to believe its contents and to obey its message. And finally, we are instructed to pass along his glorious truths to future generations so that they might grow up and never depart from that which is ultimately God-breathed. "Sanctify them through thy truth: thy word is truth" (John 17:17, KJV).

Think About It

1. Are you more spiritual or more enlightened than believers in ages past?
2. What effects did liberalism bring to Christianity?
3. Is error and schism good for the church? Why or why not?
4. Is it important for you to believe the Bible is infallible and inerrant?
5. If you hold the Bible in high regard, do you submit to *all* of its teachings?

Appendix I

Dating the Books of the Bible

THE OLD TESTAMENT

Book	Possible Dates
Genesis	*c.* 1400 – *c.* 500 BC
Exodus	*c.* 1400 – *c.* 500 BC
Leviticus	*c.* 1400 – *c.* 500 BC
Numbers	*c.* 1400 – *c.* 500 BC
Deuteronomy	*c.* 1400 – *c.* 500 BC
Joshua	*c.* 1200 – *c.* 1050 BC
Judges	*c.* 600 BC
Ruth	*c.* 1050 – *c.* 450 BC
1 Samuel	*c.* 600 BC
2 Samuel	*c.* 600 BC
1 Kings	*c.* 550 BC
2 Kings	*c.* 500 BC
1 Chronicles	*c.* 520 – *c.* 400 BC
2 Chronicles	*c.* 520 – *c.* 400 BC
Ezra	*c.* 430 – *c.* 400 BC
Nehemiah	*c.* 430 – *c.* 400 BC
Esther	*c.* 500 – *c.* 100 BC
Job	*c.* 1000 – *c.* 500 BC
Psalm	*c.* 1000 – *c.* 500 BC
Proverbs	*c.* 1000 – *c.* 450 BC
Ecclesiastes	*c.* 1000 – *c.* 600 BC
Song of Solomon	*c.* 1000 – *c.* 450 BC

THE NEW TESTAMENT

Book	Possible Dates
Matthew	AD 64–70 / 100
Mark	AD 40s / 70s
Luke	AD 63 / 75–78
John	AD 65–70 / 95
Acts	AD 62 / 130
Romans	AD 55–57
1 Corinthians	AD 55
2 Corinthians	AD 55
Galatians	AD 49
Ephesians	AD 60–62 / 70–90
Philippians	AD 61
Colossians	AD 58
1 Thessalonians	AD 50–51
2 Thessalonians	AD 51
1 Timothy	AD 62–64
2 Timothy	AD 64–65
Titus	AD 62–64
Philemon	AD 60
Hebrews	AD pre-70 / 100
James	AD 40s / late 1st century
1 Peter	AD 60s / 100
2 Peter	AD 64–65 / 110

Isaiah	*c.* 700 – *c.* 500 BC	1 John	AD 60s / 90s
Jeremiah	*c.* 585 BC	2 John	AD 60s / 130
Lamentations	*c.* 550 BC	3 John	AD 60s / 130
Ezekiel	*c.* 590 BC	Jude	AD 60s
Daniel	*c.* 600 – *c.* 200 BC	Revelation	AD pre–70 / 110
Hosea	*c.* 750 BC		
Joel	*c.* 900 – *c.* 500 BC		
Amos	*c.* 740 BC		
Obadiah	*c.* 500 BC		
Jonah	*c.* 800 – *c.* 450 BC		
Micah	*c.* 740 BC		
Nahum	*c.* 650 BC		
Habakkuk	*c.* 600 BC		
Zephaniah	*c.* 600 BC		
Haggai	*c.* 520 BC		
Zechariah	*c.* 520 BC		
Malachi	*c.* 450 BC		

Bibliography

Abanes, Richard. The *Truth Behind the Da Vinci Code: A Challenging Response to the Bestselling Novel*. Eugene: Harvest House, 2004.
Aland, Kurt and Barbara Aland. *The Text of the New Testament: an Introduction to the Critical Editions and to the Theory and Practice of Modern Textual Criticism*, trans. Erroll F. Rhodes. Grand Rapids: Eerdmans, 1987.
St. Augustine. *The City of God*, trans. Gerald G. Walsh, SJ et al. New York: Image, 1958.
———. *Confessions*, trans. Henry Chadwick. New York: Oxford University Press, 1998.
Bainton, Roland H. *Here I Stand: A Life of Martin Luther*. Nashville: Abingdon, 1978.
Barclay, William and F. F. Bruce. *The Making of the Bible*. London: Lutterworth and New York: Abingdon, 1962.
Bauer, Susan Wise. *The History of the Medieval World: From the Conversion of Constantine to the First Crusade*. New York: W. W. Norton & Company, 2010.
Beckwith, Roger T. *The Old Testament Canon of the New Testament Church: And its Background in Early Judaism*. Eugene: Wipf & Stock, 2010.
Bettenson, Henry and Chris Maunder, eds. *Documents of the Christian Church*. 3d ed. New York: Oxford University Press, 1999.
Boettner, Loraine. *Roman Catholicism*. Philipsburg: Presbyterian and Reformed, 1962.
Brown, Dan. *The Da Vinci Code*. New York: Anchor Books, 2003.
Bruce, F. F. *The Canon of Scripture*. Downers Grove: InterVarsity, 1988.
———. *The New Testament Documents: Are They Reliable?* 5th ed. Downers Grove: InterVarsity and Grand Rapids: Eerdmans, 1984.
Burer, Michael, W. Hall Harris III, and Daniel B. Wallace, eds. *New English Translation Novum Testamentum Graece*. Dallas: NET Bible Press, 2003.
Cairns, Earle E. *Christianity Through the Centuries: A History of the Christian Church*, 3d ed. Grand Rapids: Zondervan, 1996.
Chadwick, Owen. *The Pelican History of the Church: The Reformation*. Baltimore: Penguin Books, 1966.
Chamberlin, E. R. *The Bad Popes*. New York: Signet, 1971.
Comfort, Philip ed., *The Origin of the Bible*. Wheaton: Tyndale House, 2003.
Cowan, Henry. *Landmarks of Church History to the Reformation*. New York: Fleming H. Revell, no date.
Durant, Will. *The Age of Faith: A History of Medieval Civilization from Constantine to Dante A.D. 325–1300*. New York: Simon and Schuster, 1950.
Ehrman, Bart. *Misquoting Jesus: the Story Behind Who Changed the Bible and* Why. New York: HarperCollins, 2005.
Eusebius, *The History of the Church*, trans. G. A. Williamson. London: Penguin Books, 1989.
Foxe, John. *The New Foxe's Books of Martyrs*. North Brunswick: Bridge-Logos, 1997.

Geisler, Norman and Abdul Saleeb, *Answering Islam: The Crescent in the Light of the Cross*. Grand Rapids: Baker, 1993.

Gonzalez, Justo L. *The Story of Christianity: The Early Church to the Dawn of the Reformation*. New York: HarperOne, 1984.

———. *The Story of Christianity: The Reformation to the Present Day*. New York: HarperOne, 1985.

Goodspeed, Edgar J. *How Came the Bible? The Turbulent and Fascinating History of the World's Greatest Book*. Abingdon: Festival, 1976.

Greer, Thomas H. and Gavin Lewis. *A Brief History of the Western World*, 6th ed. Orlando: Harcourt Brace Jovanovich, 1968.

Herbermann, Charles, Edward Pace, Conde Pallen, Thomas Shahan, and John Wynne, eds. *The Catholic Encyclopedia: Doctrine, Discipline, and History of the Catholic Church*. Encyclopedia Press, 1915.

Herring, Judith. *The Formation of Christendom*. Princeton: Princeton University Press, 1987.

Isaacson, Walter. *Benjamin Franklin: An American Life*. New York: Simon & Schuster, 2003.

Kelly, J. N. D. *Early Christian Doctrines*. San Francisco: Harper & Row, 1978.

King, David T. *Holy Scripture: The Ground and Pillar of Our Faith*. Vol I. Battle Ground: Christian Resources, 2001.

Lasor, William, David Hubbard, and Frederic Bush. *Old Testament Survey: The Message, Form, and Background of the Old Testament*. 2d ed. Grand Rapids: Eerdmans, 1996.

Latourette, Kenneth Scott. *A History of Christianity: Reformation to the Present*. New York: Harper & Row, 1975.

Lea, Thomas, and David Black. *The New Testament: Its Background and Message*. 2d ed. Nashville: Broadman & Holman, 2003.

Livingston, James, Francis Fiorenza, Sarah Coakley, and James Evans. *Modern Christian Thought: The Enlightenment and the Nineteenth Century*. 2d ed. Minneapolis: Fortress, 2006.

Lutzer, Erwin. *The Doctrines that Divide: A Fresh Look at the Historic Doctrines That Separate Christians*. Grand Rapids: Kregel, 1998.

McElveen, Floyd. *God Word, Final, Infallible, Forever: Compelling Evidence for the Bible's Inspiration and Preservation*. Institute for Religious Research, 1985.

Metzger, Bruce. Chapters In the History of New Testament Textual Criticism. Grand Rapids: Eerdmans, 1963.

———. The Text of the New Testament: Its Transmission, Corruption, and Restoration, 3d ed. New York: Oxford University Press, 1992.

Miller, William. A Christian's Response to Islam. Phillipsburg: Presbyterian and Reformed, 1976.

Need, Stephen. *Truly Human & Truly Divine: The Story of Christ and the Seven Ecumenical Councils*. Peabody: Hendrickson, 2008.

Pache, Rene. *The Inspiration and Authority of Scripture*, trans. Helen I. Needham. Chicago: Moody, 1980.

Percival, Henry, ed. *The Seven Ecumenical Councils of the Undivided Church: Their Canons and Dogmatic Decrees, Together with the Canons of all the Local Synods Which Have Received Ecumenical Acceptance*. Grand Rapids: Eerdmans, 1974.

Placher, William C. *A History of Christian Theology*. Philadelphia: The Westminster Press, 1983.

Schaff, Philip. *A Companion to the Greek Testament and the English Version*. 4th ed. New York: Harper and Brothers, 1903.

———. *History of the Christian Church*. Grand Rapids: Eerdmans, 1979.

Schnabel, Eckhard. "History, Theology and the Biblical Canon: an Introduction to Basic Issues." *Themelios* 20.2 (1995): 16-24.

Sheldon, Henry Clay. *History of the Christian Church*. Vol 5. Peabody: Hendrickson, 1988.

Shelley, Bruce. *Church History in Plain Language*. 2d ed. Dallas: Word, 1995.

Sproul, R. C. *Chosen by God*. Wheaton: Tyndale House, 1986.

———. *Truths We Confess: A Layman's Guide to the Westminster Confession of Faith, Volume I: The Triune God*. Phillipsburg: Presbyterian and Reformed, 2006.

Tanner, J. R., C. W. Previte-Orton, Z. N. Brook. *The Cambridge Medieval History, Vol VI. Victory of the Papacy*. Cambridge: Cambridge University Press, 1929.

Walker, Williston, Richard Norris, David Lotz, and Robert Handy. *A History of the Christian Church*. 4th ed. New York: Charles Scribner's Sons, 1985.

Warfield, B. B. *An Introduction to the Textual Criticism of the New Testament*. 6th ed. London: Hodder and Stoughton, 1899.

Webster, William. *The Old Testament Canon and the Apocrypha: A Survey of the History of the Apocrypha from the Jewish Age to the Reformation*. Battle Ground: Christian Resources, 2002.

Whitaker, William. *Disputations on Holy Scripture*, trans. William Fitzgerald. Orlando: Soli Gloria, 2005.

White, James. *The King James Only Controversy: Can You Trust Modern Translations?* Minneapolis: Bethany House, 1995.

———. *The Potter's Freedom: A Defense of the Reformation and a Rebuttal of Norman Geisler's Chosen But Free*. Amityville: Calvary, 2000.

———. *The Roman Catholic Controversy: Catholics & Protestants—Do the Differences Still Matter?* Minneapolis: Bethany House, 1996.

———. *Scripture Alone: Exploring the Bible's Accuracy, Authority, and Authenticity*. Minneapolis: Bethany House, 2004.

———. *The Sovereign Grace of God: A Biblical Study of the Doctrines of Calvinism*. Lindenhurst: Great Christian Books, 2003.

www.ingramcontent.com/pod-product-compliance
Lightning Source LLC
Chambersburg PA
CBHW060822190426
43197CB00038B/2198